The UK Mediterranean Diet Cookbook for Beginners

100 Delish and Easy Recipes with Color Pictures and 30-Day Meal Plan to Eat Well and Develop A Healthy Lifestyle (Colour Edition)

Peter Nealson

Copyright © 2025 By Peter Nealson
All rights reserved.

No part of this book may be reproduced, transmitted, or distributed in any form or by any means without permission in writing from the publisher except in the case of brief quotations embodied in critical articles or reviews.

Legal & Disclaimer

The content and information in this book is consistent and truthful, and it has been provided for informational, educational and business purposes only.

The illustrations in the book are from the website shutterstock.com, depositphoto.com and freepik.com and have been authorized.

The content and information contained in this book has been compiled from reliable sources, which are accurate based on the knowledge, belief, expertise and information of the Author. The author cannot be held liable for any omissions and/or errors.

Table of Content

Introduction ·· 1

Chapter 1: The Mediterranean Diet 101 ························ 2

Chapter 2: Breakfast ·· 7

Chapter 3: Vegetarian and Vegan Dishes ···················· 14

Chapter 4: Fish and Seafood ······································ 21

Chapter 5: Meat and Poultry ······································ 28

Chapter 6: Pasta and Salads ······································ 36

Chapter 7: Soups and Stews ······································ 43

Chapter 8: Beans and Grains ····································· 50

Chapter 9: Starters & Snacks ····································· 57

Chapter 10: Desserts & Drinks ··································· 64

Appendix 1: Measurement Conversion Chart ················ 71

Appendix 2: 30-Day Meal Plan ····································· 72

Appendix 3: Recipes Index ·· 74

INTRODUCTION

Welcome to the sun-drenched flavours of the Mediterranean! Our journey through this storied region is not just a culinary adventure, but a lifestyle embraced by those fortunate enough to live along its azure coasts. The Mediterranean Diet, celebrated for its vibrant ingredients and numerous health benefits, represents a centuries-old tradition of eating that is both sustainable and delightfully delicious.

In this book, we explore the essence of Mediterranean eating, which is rooted in dishes that are as nutritious as they are enticing. Central to this diet are the abundant use of olive oil, fresh fruits and vegetables, hearty grains, and the occasional indulgence in fish and poultry. It's a testament to a way of life that prioritises wellness and enjoyment in every meal.

From the lush groves of olive trees in Spain to the bustling markets of Istanbul, the Mediterranean Diet is as diverse as the cultures that flank the Mediterranean Sea. Each recipe in this collection has been tailored to suit a British palate while remaining true to its origins. This means accessible ingredients and simplified techniques that do not compromise on taste or authenticity.

Moreover, the Mediterranean Diet is more than just a list of foods; it's a holistic approach to eating that encourages cooking with family, sharing meals with friends, and slowing down to savour each bite. In embracing these practices, we invite not only the flavours but also the spirit of the Mediterranean into our homes.

Prepare to be transported by the robust flavours of Sicilian caponata, the aromatic allure of Moroccan tagines, and the simple pleasure of Greek meze. Whether you are a seasoned chef or a curious novice, these recipes will inspire you to embrace a healthier, happier way of eating.

Welcome aboard this culinary voyage—a taste of the Mediterranean awaits.

Chapter 1: The Mediterranean Diet 101

The Mediterranean Diet is a renowned and time-honored approach to eating that takes inspiration from the traditional dietary patterns of Mediterranean countries. It embodies a holistic and balanced lifestyle, promoting not only physical health but also social connections and a deep appreciation for food.

At its core, the Mediterranean Diet revolves around wholesome, unprocessed foods that are rich in nutrients and flavours. The diet emphasizes a wide variety of plant-based foods, including fruits, vegetables, whole grains, legumes, nuts, and seeds. These ingredients form the foundation of meals, providing an abundance of vitamins, minerals, fibre, and antioxidants.

Healthy fats are another cornerstone of the Mediterranean Diet, with olive oil taking centre stage. Olive oil, known for its heart-healthy properties, is used generously in cooking and as a flavourful drizzle over dishes. Fish and seafood are also celebrated sources of lean protein and beneficial omega-3 fatty acids within the diet.

The Mediterranean Diet encourages moderation in the consumption of dairy products, poultry, and eggs. Red meat is limited and reserved for occasional enjoyment. Additionally, the diet embraces the vibrant flavours of herbs and spices, allowing for a reduced reliance on salt for seasoning.

More than just a list of foods, the Mediterranean Diet represents a mindful and communal approach to eating. Meals are savoured and enjoyed in the company of others, fostering a sense of connection and well-being. Regular physical activity, such as walking and other forms of exercise, is also encouraged as an integral part of the Mediterranean lifestyle.

Numerous studies have highlighted the health benefits associated with the Mediterranean Diet. It has been linked to a reduced risk of heart disease, certain cancers, and chronic conditions like diabetes and obesity. Furthermore, the diet's emphasis on whole foods and nutrient-dense ingredients supports weight management and overall longevity.

The Mediterranean Diet is a celebration of simplicity, balance, and the joy of nourishing oneself with wholesome foods. By embracing its principles, individuals can embark on a flavourful and healthful journey that promotes well-being, culinary exploration, and a deep connection to the rich Mediterranean heritage.

Background of the Mediterranean Diet

The Mediterranean Diet is deeply rooted in the cultural and historical heritage of the Mediterranean region, which spans countries like Greece, Italy, Spain, and Morocco, among others. It reflects the dietary patterns and traditions that have been passed down through generations, shaped by the geography, climate, and cultural influences of the Mediterranean basin.

The origins of the Mediterranean Diet can be traced back thousands of years. It is believed to have been shaped by the agricultural practices and culinary customs of ancient civilizations, including the Greeks, Romans, and Phoenicians. These societies cultivated a diverse array of fruits, vegetables, grains, and legumes, as well as domesticated animals for meat and dairy products.

The Mediterranean region's favorable climate and fertile soil have played a significant role in shaping the diet. Abundant sunshine, a temperate climate, and proximity to the sea have provided favorable conditions for growing a wide variety of fresh produce, including olives, citrus fruits, grapes, and an assortment of vegetables.

Historically, the Mediterranean Diet was not just about the selection of foods but also the way they were prepared, shared, and enjoyed. It was characterised by the use of local, seasonal ingredients and traditional cooking techniques, often involving simple methods such as grilling, roasting, and stewing. Fresh herbs and spices, such as oregano, thyme, rosemary, and saffron, were employed to enhance flavours.

Beyond the culinary aspect, the Mediterranean Diet has deep cultural and social significance. Meals are viewed as a communal and social event, bringing family and friends together around the table. It is a time for shared conversation, storytelling, and a sense of connection. The Mediterranean lifestyle encourages a relaxed and unhurried approach to eating, allowing individuals to savour each bite and appreciate the pleasures of food and company.

The cultural and historical significance of the Mediterranean Diet has attracted attention from researchers and health professionals. In the mid-20th century, the Seven Countries Study conducted by Dr. Ancel Keys brought international recognition to the diet's health benefits, particularly its association with reduced rates of heart disease in Mediterranean populations.

Today, the Mediterranean Diet has transcended borders and gained global popularity as a model for healthy eating. Its emphasis on whole foods, plant-based ingredients, and healthy fats has been widely recognized and recommended by nutritionists and health organizations worldwide.

The cultural and historical background of the Mediterranean Diet provides valuable insights into the rich tapestry of traditions, flavours, and practices that have shaped this dietary pattern. Embracing the Mediterranean Diet is not just about nourishing the body but also appreciating the cultural heritage and wisdom that it encompasses.

Health Benefits of the Mediterranean Diet

The Mediterranean Diet is celebrated for its numerous health benefits, which have been extensively studied and documented. This dietary pattern, inspired by the eating habits of Mediterranean countries, offers a holistic approach to nutrition that promotes overall well-being. Here are some of the notable health benefits associated with the Mediterranean Diet:

- **Reduced Risk of Heart Disease**

The Mediterranean Diet has been consistently linked to a lower risk of heart disease. It emphasizes heart-healthy fats, such as monounsaturated fats found in olive oil and omega-3 fatty acids from fish, which can help improve cholesterol levels, reduce inflammation, and support cardiovascular health.

- **Improved Brain Health**

Following the Mediterranean Diet has shown promising effects on brain health and may help reduce the risk of cognitive decline and neurodegenerative diseases like Alzheimer's. The diet's emphasis on antioxidant-rich foods, including fruits, vegetables, and herbs, along with healthy fats, may play a role in preserving brain function.

- **Lowered Risk of Type 2 Diabetes**

Adopting the Mediterranean Diet has been associated with a decreased risk of developing type 2 diabetes. The diet's emphasis on whole grains, legumes, fruits, and vegetables, along with healthy fats, helps regulate blood sugar levels and improve insulin sensitivity.

- **Weight Management**

The Mediterranean Diet offers a balanced approach to weight management. Its focus on whole, nutrient-dense foods, coupled with portion control and mindful eating, can support healthy weight loss or maintenance. The diet's high fibre content and inclusion of lean proteins help promote satiety and reduce the likelihood of overeating.

- **Reduced Risk of Certain Cancers**

Research suggests that adhering to the Mediterranean Diet may lower the risk of certain cancers, particularly colorectal, breast, and prostate cancers. The diet's abundant intake of plant-based foods, antioxidants, and anti-inflammatory compounds may contribute to its protective effects.

- **Improved Longevity**

Following the Mediterranean Diet has been associated with increased longevity and a lower risk of premature death. Its nutrient-dense foods, healthy fats, and overall dietary pattern have been linked to improved overall health and a reduced risk of chronic diseases, leading to a longer and healthier life.

- **Enhanced Nutritional Status**

The Mediterranean Diet provides a rich array of essential nutrients, including vitamins, minerals, fibre, and antioxidants. It emphasizes whole foods, limiting processed and refined products, which helps ensure a well-rounded and balanced nutrient intake.

- **Positive Mental Health**

The Mediterranean Diet's focus on whole foods and nutrients may have a positive impact on mental health. Some studies suggest that adherence to the diet is associated with a reduced risk of depression and improved overall mental well-being.

It's important to note that the health benefits of the Mediterranean Diet are not solely attributed to individual foods but to the overall dietary pattern and lifestyle it promotes. By embracing the principles of the Mediterranean Diet, individuals can enjoy a delicious and varied range of foods while reaping the rewards of improved health and vitality.

Key Principles of the Mediterranean Diet

Celebrated for its diverse range of flavours, abundance of fresh ingredients, and health-promoting properties, the Mediterranean Diet offers a holistic and sustainable way of nourishing the body. Embracing the essence of Mediterranean living, the key principles of this dietary pattern include:

- **Abundance of Plant-Based Foods**

The Mediterranean Diet places a strong emphasis on consuming a variety of plant-based foods, including fruits, vegetables, whole grains, legumes, nuts, and seeds. These foods provide essential nutrients, fibre, and antioxidants that contribute to overall health and well-being.

- **Healthy Fats**

Healthy fats, particularly monounsaturated fats found in olive oil, are a prominent feature of the Mediterranean Diet. These fats help to maintain heart health and provide satiety. Other sources of healthy fats in the diet include avocados, nuts, and seeds.

- **Moderate Consumption of Fish and Poultry**

The Mediterranean Diet encourages moderate consumption of fish, especially fatty fish like salmon, mackerel, and sardines, which are rich in omega-3 fatty acids. Poultry is also included in moderation, while red meat is limited.

- **Limited Intake of Red Meat and Sweets**

The Mediterranean Diet recommends limiting the consumption of red meat to occasional indulgences and suggests avoiding processed meats. Sweets and sugary treats are also kept to a minimum.

- **Dairy Products in Moderation**

Dairy products, such as yogurt and cheese, are a part of the Mediterranean Diet but are consumed in moderation. They can provide calcium, protein, and other essential nutrients.

- **Flavourful Herbs and Spices**

The Mediterranean Diet embraces the use of herbs and spices to enhance the flavour of dishes, reducing the need for excess salt. Commonly used herbs and spices include garlic, oregano, basil, rosemary, and cinnamon.

- **Red Wine in Moderation**

While not a requirement, moderate consumption of red wine is often associated with the Mediterranean Diet. It is typically enjoyed in moderation and with meals. However, it is important to note that excessive alcohol consumption can have negative health effects.

- **Regular Physical Activity**

The Mediterranean Diet is complemented by an active lifestyle. Regular physical activity, such as walking, gardening, or engaging in sports, is encouraged to promote overall health and well-being.

By adhering to these key principles, individuals can adopt a balanced and sustainable approach to eating that encompasses the essence of the Mediterranean Diet. These principles emphasize whole, unprocessed foods, mindful eating, and an active lifestyle, allowing for a lifelong commitment to health and vitality.

Nutritional Components of the Mediterranean Diet

The Mediterranean Diet encompasses a balanced intake of various essential nutritional components, ensuring a well-rounded approach to nourishment. Key components of the Mediterranean Diet include:

* **Carbohydrates:** The diet emphasizes the consumption of complex carbohydrates, primarily derived from whole grains, legumes, fruits, and vegetables. These carbohydrates provide a sustained source of energy and are rich in fibre, vitamins, and minerals.

* **Protein:** The Mediterranean Diet incorporates moderate amounts of protein from various sources. While plant-based proteins like legumes, nuts, and seeds are emphasized, moderate consumption of poultry, fish, and dairy products is also included. This provides a diverse range of essential amino acids for building and repairing tissues.

* **Fats:** The Mediterranean Diet promotes the consumption of healthy fats, particularly monounsaturated fats found in olive oil and avocados. These fats offer benefits for heart health and provide a source of energy. Additionally, omega-3 fatty acids from sources like fatty fish, flaxseeds, and walnuts are included for their anti-inflammatory properties.

* **Fibre:** The diet is rich in dietary fibre due to the emphasis on whole grains, legumes, fruits, and vegetables. Fibre aids in digestion, promotes satiety, and helps maintain healthy blood sugar levels.

* **Vitamins and Minerals:** The Mediterranean Diet naturally provides a wide range of vitamins and minerals through the consumption of nutrient-dense foods. Fruits, vegetables, whole grains, legumes, nuts, and seeds offer a variety of vitamins (such as vitamin C, vitamin A, and folate) and minerals (such as potassium, magnesium, and calcium).

By prioritizing these key nutritional components, the Mediterranean Diet offers a well-balanced and nourishing approach to eating, supporting overall health and well-being.

Practical Tips for Adopting the Mediterranean Diet

Here are some practical tips for adopting the Mediterranean Diet, including balanced meals, pantry essentials, and meal prep:

1. Create Balanced Meals

Aim to include a variety of food groups in each meal to ensure a balanced nutritional profile. Include a source of lean protein (such as fish, poultry, legumes, or tofu), whole grains (like brown rice or quinoa), plenty of vegetables, and a serving of healthy fats (like olive oil or nuts).

2. Stock a Mediterranean Pantry

Keep your pantry well-stocked with Mediterranean essentials such as extra virgin olive oil, canned tomatoes, whole grains, legumes, dried herbs and spices, and a variety of nuts and seeds. Having these ingredients on hand makes it easier to whip up Mediterranean-inspired meals.

3. Understand Macronutrients

Pay attention to the macronutrient composition of your meals. Aim for a balance of carbohydrates, proteins, and healthy fats. This balance helps provide sustained energy, promotes satiety, and supports overall health.

4. Practice Meal Prep

Dedicate some time each week to meal prep. Plan and prepare meals and snacks in advance, portioning them into containers for easy grab-and-go options. This helps you stay on track with your Mediterranean Diet goals and prevents resorting to unhealthy food choices when you're busy or short on time.

5. Practice Portion Control

While the Mediterranean Diet focuses on wholesome foods, portion control is still essential for maintaining a healthy weight. Use smaller plates and bowls to help control portion sizes, and listen to your body's hunger and fullness cues.

6. Enjoy Social Meals

The Mediterranean Diet is not just about the food; it's also about the social aspect of dining. Gather with friends and family to share meals, engage in conversations, and enjoy the overall experience of eating together.

7. Prioritize Plant-Based Foods

Make plant-based foods the centrepiece of your meals. Fill your plate with colourful fruits, vegetables, whole grains, legumes, and nuts. These plant-based foods provide a wide array of nutrients, fibre, and antioxidants.

8. Include Healthy Snacks

Keep a variety of healthy snacks readily available, such as cut-up fruits and vegetables, Greek yogurt, hummus with wholemeal crackers, or a handful of nuts. These options help you satisfy cravings between meals while sticking to the principles of the Mediterranean Diet.

9. Prioritize Physical Activity

Alongside following the Mediterranean Diet, engaging in regular physical activity is essential for overall health and well-being. Incorporate activities you enjoy, such as brisk walking, swimming, cycling, or dancing, into your daily routine. Aim for at least 150 minutes of moderate-intensity aerobic exercise or 75 minutes of vigorous-intensity exercise per week, as recommended by health guidelines.

By incorporating these practical tips into your lifestyle, you can successfully adopt the Mediterranean Diet and reap its numerous health benefits. Remember, the key is to make gradual changes that are sustainable and work for you.

CHAPTER 2
Breakfast

Avocado and Tomato on Wholemeal Toast ·········· 8

Mediterranean Vegetable Frittata ·········· 8

Smoked Salmon and Soft Cheese Bagel ·········· 9

Mediterranean Chickpea Pancakes ·········· 9

Roasted Tomato and Basil Porridge ·········· 10

Spinach and Feta Omelette ·········· 10

Tomato and Olive Breakfast Muffins ·········· 11

Mediterranean-style Scrambled Eggs ·········· 11

Roasted Pepper and Goat's Cheese Toast ·········· 12

Aubergine and Red Pepper Shakshuka ·········· 12

Courgette and Ricotta Tart ·········· 13

Mediterranean Breakfast Quinoa ·········· 13

Avocado and Tomato on Wholemeal Toast

Serves: 2

|PREP TIME: 5 minutes
|COOK TIME: 5 minutes

2 slices of wholemeal bread
1 ripe avocado
1 medium tomato, sliced
1 tbsp. lemon juice
Salt and black pepper, to taste
1 tbsp. fresh basil, chopped

1. Toast the slices of wholemeal bread.
2. While the bread is toasting, scoop the avocado into a bowl and mash it with the lemon juice.
3. Spread the mashed avocado evenly over the toasted bread slices.
4. Arrange the tomato slices on top of the avocado.
5. Season with salt and black pepper, and sprinkle with fresh basil.
6. Serve immediately.

Nutrition Info per Serving:

Calories: 220, Protein: 4 g, Fat: 14 g, Carbohydrates: 20 g, Fibre: 7 g, Sugar: 2 g, Sodium: 170 mg

Mediterranean Vegetable Frittata

Serves: 4-6

|PREP TIME: 10 minutes
|COOK TIME: 25 minutes

1 tbsp. olive oil
1 red onion, finely sliced
1 red pepper, chopped
1 courgette, sliced
8 cherry tomatoes, halved
6 large eggs
50 g feta cheese, crumbled
2 tbsps. fresh parsley, chopped
Salt and black pepper, to taste

1. Preheat the oven to 180°C.
2. Heat the olive oil in an ovenproof frying pan over medium heat. Add the onion, red pepper, and courgette, and sauté until softened, about 5 minutes.
3. Add the cherry tomatoes and cook for another 2 minutes.
4. In a bowl, beat the eggs and season with salt and black pepper.
5. Pour the eggs into the frying pan, ensuring the vegetables are evenly distributed.
6. Sprinkle the feta cheese and parsley over the top.
7. Transfer the frying pan to the oven and bake for 15-20 minutes, until the frittata is set and golden on top.
8. Slice and serve warm.

Nutrition Info per Serving:

Calories: 120, Protein: 10 g, Fat: 8 g, Carbohydrates: 5 g, Fibre: 1 g, Sugar: 3 g, Sodium: 220 mg

Smoked Salmon and Soft Cheese Bagel

Serves: 2

2 wholemeal bagels
100 g smoked salmon
100 g light soft cheese
1 tbsp. capers
1 small red onion, thinly sliced
1 tbsp. fresh dill, chopped
Lemon wedges, to serve

|PREP TIME: 10 minutes
|COOK TIME: 5 minutes

1. Slice the bagels in half and toast them until golden.
2. Spread the soft cheese evenly on each bagel half.
3. Top with smoked salmon, capers, and red onion slices.
4. Garnish with fresh dill.
5. Serve with lemon wedges on the side.

Nutrition Info per Serving:

Calories: 280, Protein: 16 g, Fat: 12 g, Carbohydrates: 28 g, Fibre: 3 g, Sugar: 4 g, Sodium: 560 mg

Mediterranean Chickpea Pancakes

Serves: 4

200 g chickpea flour
300 ml water
1 tbsp. olive oil
1 tsp. salt
1 red pepper, finely chopped
1 small courgette, grated
2 spring onions, chopped
2 tbsps. fresh parsley, chopped
Black pepper, to taste

|PREP TIME: 10 minutes
|COOK TIME: 15 minutes

1. In a large bowl, whisk together the chickpea flour, water, olive oil, and salt until smooth.
2. Stir in the chopped red pepper, grated courgette, spring onions, and parsley.
3. Heat a non-stick frying pan over medium heat and lightly oil it.
4. Pour a ladleful of the batter into the pan and spread it out to form a pancake.
5. Cook for 3-4 minutes on each side, until golden and cooked through.
6. Repeat with the remaining batter.
7. Serve warm, seasoned with black pepper.

Nutrition Info per Serving:

Calories: 180, Protein: 8 g, Fat: 5 g, Carbohydrates: 25 g, Fibre: 5 g, Sugar: 3 g, Sodium: 350 mg

Roasted Tomato and Basil Porridge

Serves: 2

|PREP TIME: 5 minutes
|COOK TIME: 20 minutes

100 g porridge oats
300 ml water or milk
1 tbsp. olive oil
150 g cherry tomatoes, halved
1 tbsp. fresh basil, chopped
Salt and black pepper, to taste

1. Preheat the oven to 200°C.
2. Place the cherry tomatoes on a baking tray, drizzle with olive oil, and roast for 15 minutes.
3. In a saucepan, bring the water or milk to a boil. Add the oats and cook for 5 minutes, stirring occasionally.
4. Stir in the roasted tomatoes and fresh basil.
5. Season with salt and black pepper.
6. Serve warm.

Nutrition Info per Serving:

Calories: 220, Protein: 6 g, Fat: 9 g, Carbohydrates: 29 g, Fibre: 5 g, Sugar: 7 g, Sodium: 150 mg

Spinach and Feta Omelette

Serves: 1

|PREP TIME: 5 minutes
|COOK TIME: 5-10 minutes

2 large eggs
1 tbsp. milk
1 tsp. olive oil
50 g spinach, chopped
30 g feta cheese, crumbled
Salt and black pepper, to taste

1. In a bowl, beat the eggs with the milk, and season with salt and black pepper.
2. Heat the olive oil in a non-stick frying pan over medium heat.
3. Add the spinach and cook until wilted, about 2 minutes.
4. Pour the egg mixture into the pan, tilting to ensure even coverage.
5. Cook for 2-3 minutes, until the eggs are nearly set.
6. Sprinkle the feta cheese over one half of the omelette.
7. Fold the omelette in half and cook for another minute, until the cheese is slightly melted.
8. Serve warm.

Nutrition Info per Serving:

Calories: 210, Protein: 14 g, Fat: 15 g, Carbohydrates: 3 g, Fibre: 1 g, Sugar: 1 g, Sodium: 320 mg

Tomato and Olive Breakfast Muffins

Serves: 6

150 g wholemeal flour
1 tsp. baking powder
½ tsp. bicarbonate of soda
½ tsp. salt
2 large eggs
200 ml natural yoghurt
2 tbsps. olive oil
100 g cherry tomatoes, chopped
50 g black olives, sliced
50 g feta cheese, crumbled
2 tbsps. fresh basil, chopped

PREP TIME: 15 minutes
COOK TIME: 25 minutes

1. Preheat the oven to 180°C and line a muffin tin with paper cases.
2. In a large bowl, combine the wholemeal flour, baking powder, bicarbonate of soda, and salt.
3. In another bowl, whisk together the eggs, yoghurt, and olive oil.
4. Add the wet ingredients to the dry ingredients and mix until just combined.
5. Fold in the chopped cherry tomatoes, sliced olives, feta cheese, and basil.
6. Divide the batter evenly among the muffin cases.
7. Bake for 20-25 minutes, until a skewer inserted into the centre comes out clean.
8. Allow to cool slightly before serving.

Nutrition Info per Serving:

Calories: 150, Protein: 6 g, Fat: 8 g, Carbohydrates: 15 g, Fibre: 2 g, Sugar: 2 g, Sodium: 300 mg

Mediterranean-style Scrambled Eggs

Serves: 2

4 large eggs
1 tbsp. milk
1 tbsp. olive oil
1 small tomato, chopped
50 g spinach, chopped
30 g feta cheese, crumbled
Salt and black pepper, to taste

PREP TIME: 5 minutes
COOK TIME: 5 minutes

1. In a bowl, whisk the eggs with the milk, and season with salt and black pepper.
2. Heat the olive oil in a non-stick frying pan over medium heat.
3. Add the tomato and spinach, and cook until the spinach is wilted, about 2 minutes.
4. Pour the egg mixture into the pan and cook, stirring gently, until the eggs are softly scrambled.
5. Sprinkle the feta cheese over the eggs and stir until just combined.
6. Serve immediately.

Nutrition Info per Serving:

Calories: 210, Protein: 14 g, Fat: 15 g, Carbohydrates: 3 g, Fibre: 1 g, Sugar: 2 g, Sodium: 340 mg

CHAPTER 2
Breakfast

Roasted Pepper and Goat's Cheese Toast

Serves: 2

PREP TIME: 10 minutes
COOK TIME: 10 minutes

2 slices of wholemeal bread
1 red pepper
1 yellow pepper
1 tbsp. olive oil
50 g goat's cheese
1 tbsp. fresh basil, chopped
Salt and black pepper, to taste

1. Preheat the oven to 200°C.
2. Cut the peppers into strips and place them on a baking tray. Drizzle with olive oil and roast for 10 minutes.
3. Toast the bread slices.
4. Spread the goat's cheese evenly over the toasted bread.
5. Top with the roasted pepper strips.
6. Sprinkle with fresh basil and season with salt and black pepper.
7. Serve warm.

Nutrition Info per Serving:

Calories: 190, Protein: 6 g, Fat: 10 g, Carbohydrates: 18 g, Fibre: 3 g, Sugar: 4 g, Sodium: 220 mg

Aubergine and Red Pepper Shakshuka

Serves: 4

PREP TIME: 10 minutes
COOK TIME: 25 minutes

1 tbsp. olive oil
1 aubergine, diced
1 red pepper, chopped
1 onion, finely chopped
2 garlic cloves, minced
400 g tinned tomatoes
1 tsp. ground cumin
1 tsp. smoked paprika
4 large eggs
Salt and black pepper, to taste
Fresh coriander, chopped (optional)

1. Heat the olive oil in a large frying pan over medium heat. Add the aubergine, red pepper, and onion, and sauté until softened, about 10 minutes.
2. Add the garlic, cumin, and smoked paprika, and cook for another minute.
3. Pour in the tinned tomatoes, season with salt and black pepper, and simmer for 10 minutes until the sauce thickens.
4. Make four wells in the sauce and crack an egg into each well.
5. Cover the pan and cook for 5-7 minutes until the eggs are set to your liking.
6. Sprinkle with fresh coriander, if using, and serve hot.

Nutrition Info per Serving:

Calories: 200, Protein: 10 g, Fat: 12 g, Carbohydrates: 15 g, Fibre: 6 g, Sugar: 8 g, Sodium: 340 mg

CHAPTER 2
Breakfast

Courgette and Ricotta Tart

Serves: 4

1 ready-rolled puff pastry sheet
250 g ricotta cheese
2 courgettes, thinly sliced
1 tbsp. olive oil
1 tbsp. fresh thyme, chopped
Salt and black pepper, to taste

|PREP TIME: 15 minutes
|COOK TIME: 25-30 minutes

1. Preheat the oven to 200°C.
2. Place the puff pastry sheet on a baking tray.
3. Spread the ricotta cheese evenly over the pastry, leaving a 2 cm border around the edges.
4. Arrange the courgette slices on top of the ricotta.
5. Drizzle with olive oil and sprinkle with fresh thyme, salt, and black pepper.
6. Fold the edges of the pastry over to create a border.
7. Bake for 25-30 minutes, until the pastry is golden and crisp.
8. Serve warm.

Nutrition Info per Serving:

Calories: 290, Protein: 9 g, Fat: 18 g, Carbohydrates: 23 g, Fibre: 2 g, Sugar: 3 g, Sodium: 250 mg

Mediterranean Breakfast Quinoa

Serves: 2

100 g quinoa, rinsed
200 ml water
1 tbsp. olive oil
1 baby cucumber, diced
1 small red onion, finely chopped
100 g cherry tomatoes, halved
50 g feta cheese, crumbled
2 tbsps. fresh parsley, chopped
1 tbsp. lemon juice
Salt and black pepper, to taste

|PREP TIME: 5 minutes
|COOK TIME: 15 minutes

1. In a saucepan, bring the water to a boil. Add the quinoa, reduce the heat, and simmer for 15 minutes, until the water is absorbed and the quinoa is tender.
2. Fluff the quinoa with a fork and transfer to a large bowl.
3. Stir in the olive oil, cucumber, red onion, cherry tomatoes, feta cheese, parsley, and lemon juice.
4. Season with salt and black pepper, and mix well.
5. Serve warm or cold.

Nutrition Info per Serving:

Calories: 250, Protein: 9 g, Fat: 11 g, Carbohydrates: 28 g, Fibre: 5 g, Sugar: 4 g, Sodium: 200 mg

CHAPTER 2
Breakfast

CHAPTER 3
Vegetarian and Vegan Dishes

Mediterranean Stuffed Peppers ········· 15

Vegan Moussaka ········· 15

Butternut Squash and Chickpea Tagine ········· 16

Grilled Vegetable Skewers with Tzatziki ········· 16

Mediterranean Stuffed Tomatoes ········· 17

Lentil and Vegetable Soup ········· 17

Stuffed Aubergines with Quinoa ········· 18

Mushroom and Thyme Spelt ········· 18

Grilled Aubergine Rolls ········· 19

Vegan Mediterranean Pizza ········· 19

Courgette and Tomato Gratin ········· 20

Roasted Vegetable Couscous ········· 20

Mediterranean Stuffed Peppers

Serves: 4

4 large red peppers
200 g quinoa
1 tbsp. olive oil
1 onion, finely chopped
2 garlic cloves, minced
1 courgette, diced

1 tin of chopped tomatoes (400 g)
1 tsp. dried oregano
1 tsp. dried basil
50 g black olives, sliced
Salt and black pepper, to taste
Fresh parsley, chopped (for garnish)

PREP TIME: 15 minutes
COOK TIME: 35-40 minutes

1. Preheat the oven to 200°C.
2. Cut the tops off the peppers and remove the seeds.
3. Cook the quinoa according to the package instructions and set aside.
4. In a large frying pan, heat the olive oil over medium heat. Add the onion and garlic and sauté until softened, about 5 minutes.
5. Add the courgette and cook for another 5 minutes.
6. Stir in the chopped tomatoes, cooked quinoa, oregano, basil, and olives. Season with salt and black pepper.
7. Stuff the peppers with the quinoa mixture and place them in a baking dish.
8. Bake for 25-30 minutes, until the peppers are tender.
9. Garnish with fresh parsley and serve hot.

Nutrition Info per Serving:

Calories: 210, Protein: 6 g, Fat: 7 g, Carbohydrates: 30 g, Fibre: 8 g, Sugar: 10 g, Sodium: 260 mg

Vegan Moussaka

Serves: 6-8

2 large aubergines, sliced
3 potatoes, peeled and sliced
1 tbsp. olive oil
1 onion, finely chopped
2 garlic cloves, minced
400 g tinned lentils, drained

400 g chopped tomatoes
1 tsp. ground cinnamon
1 tsp. dried oregano
50 g vegan cheese, grated (optional)
Salt and black pepper, to taste

PREP TIME: 20 minutes
COOK TIME: 45 minutes

1. Preheat the oven to 180°C.
2. Lay the aubergine and potato slices on a baking tray, drizzle with olive oil, and roast for 20 minutes, until tender.
3. Meanwhile, heat the olive oil in a frying pan over medium heat. Add the onion and garlic, and sauté until softened, about 5 minutes.
4. Add the lentils, chopped tomatoes, cinnamon, and oregano. Season with salt and black pepper. Simmer for 10 minutes.
5. In a baking dish, layer the roasted potatoes, aubergines, and lentil mixture.
6. Top with grated vegan cheese, if using.
7. Bake for 25 minutes, until golden and bubbly.
8. Serve hot.

Nutrition Info per Serving:

Calories: 230, Protein: 7 g, Fat: 8 g, Carbohydrates: 33 g, Fibre: 10 g, Sugar: 8 g, Sodium: 240 mg

Butternut Squash and Chickpea Tagine

Serves: 4-6

|PREP TIME: 20 minutes
|COOK TIME: 35 minutes

1 tbsp. olive oil
1 onion, finely chopped
2 garlic cloves, minced
1 butternut squash, peeled and cubed
1 tin of chickpeas (400 g), drained and rinsed
400 g tinned tomatoes
1 tsp. ground cumin
1 tsp. ground cinnamon
1 tsp. ground coriander
200 ml vegetable stock
Salt and black pepper, to taste
Fresh coriander, chopped (for garnish)

1. Heat the olive oil in a large pot over medium heat. Add the onion and garlic, and sauté until softened, about 5 minutes.
2. Stir in the ground cumin, ground cinnamon, and ground coriander, and cook for another minute.
3. Add the butternut squash, chickpeas, tinned tomatoes, and vegetable stock. Season with salt and black pepper.
4. Bring to a boil, then reduce the heat and simmer for 30 minutes, until the butternut squash is tender.
5. Garnish with fresh coriander and serve hot.

Nutrition Info per Serving:

Calories: 230, Protein: 6 g, Fat: 7 g, Carbohydrates: 36 g, Fibre: 8 g, Sugar: 10 g, Sodium: 300 mg

Grilled Vegetable Skewers with Tzatziki

Serves: 4

|PREP TIME: 20 minutes
|COOK TIME: 10 minutes

1 courgette, sliced
1 red pepper, chopped
1 yellow pepper, chopped
1 red onion, cut into wedges
1 tbsp. olive oil
Salt and black pepper, to taste
200 g Greek yoghurt
½ cucumber, grated
1 garlic clove, minced
1 tbsp. lemon juice
1 tbsp. fresh dill, chopped

1. Preheat the grill to medium-high heat.
2. Thread the courgette, red pepper, yellow pepper, and red onion onto skewers.
3. Brush the vegetables with olive oil and season with salt and black pepper.
4. Grill the skewers for 8-10 minutes, turning occasionally, until the vegetables are tender and slightly charred.
5. Meanwhile, in a bowl, combine the Greek yoghurt, grated cucumber, garlic, lemon juice, and dill. Mix well.
6. Serve the vegetable skewers with tzatziki on the side.

Nutrition Info per Serving:

Calories: 160, Protein: 6 g, Fat: 8 g, Carbohydrates: 14 g, Fibre: 3 g, Sugar: 7 g, Sodium: 120 mg

CHAPTER 3
Vegetarian and Vegan Dishes

Mediterranean Stuffed Tomatoes

Serves: 4

4 large tomatoes
200 g couscous
1 tbsp. olive oil
1 onion, finely chopped
2 garlic cloves, minced
100 g spinach, chopped
1 red pepper, diced
1 tsp. dried oregano
1 tsp. dried basil
Salt and black pepper, to taste
Fresh parsley, chopped (for garnish)

|PREP TIME: 15 minutes
|COOK TIME: 40 minutes

1. Preheat the oven to 200°C.
2. Cut the tops off the tomatoes and scoop out the insides, setting them aside. Place the hollowed tomatoes in a baking dish.
3. Cook the couscous according to the package instructions and set aside.
4. In a frying pan, heat the olive oil over medium heat. Add the onion and garlic and sauté until softened, about 5 minutes.
5. Add the spinach, red pepper, and the scooped-out tomato insides, and cook for another 5 minutes.
6. Stir in the cooked couscous, oregano, and basil. Season with salt and black pepper.
7. Stuff the tomatoes with the couscous mixture and place the tops back on.
8. Bake for 25-30 minutes, until the tomatoes are tender.
9. Garnish with fresh parsley and serve hot.

Nutrition Info per Serving:

Calories: 190, Protein: 5 g, Fat: 7 g, Carbohydrates: 28 g, Fibre: 6 g, Sugar: 10 g, Sodium: 280 mg

Lentil and Vegetable Soup

Serves: 4

1 tbsp. olive oil
1 onion, finely chopped
2 garlic cloves, minced
2 carrots, chopped
2 celery sticks, chopped
200 g red lentils
1 tin of chopped tomatoes (400 g)
1 litre vegetable stock
1 tsp. ground cumin
1 tsp. smoked paprika
Salt and black pepper, to taste
Fresh parsley, chopped (for garnish)

|PREP TIME: 10 minutes
|COOK TIME: 30 minutes

1. In a large pot, heat the olive oil over medium heat. Add the onion and garlic and sauté until softened, about 5 minutes.
2. Add the carrots and celery, and cook for another 5 minutes.
3. Stir in the red lentils, chopped tomatoes, vegetable stock, ground cumin, and smoked paprika. Season with salt and black pepper.
4. Bring to a boil, then reduce the heat and simmer for 20 minutes, until the lentils and vegetables are tender.
5. Garnish with fresh parsley and serve hot.

Nutrition Info per Serving:

Calories: 250, Protein: 12 g, Fat: 6 g, Carbohydrates: 36 g, Fibre: 12 g, Sugar: 9 g, Sodium: 380 mg

Stuffed Aubergines with Quinoa

Serves: 4

|PREP TIME: 15 minutes
|COOK TIME: 40 minutes

2 large aubergines
200 g quinoa
1 tbsp. olive oil
1 onion, finely chopped
2 garlic cloves, minced
1 tin of chopped tomatoes (400 g)
1 tsp. dried oregano
1 tsp. dried basil
50 g black olives, sliced
Salt and black pepper, to taste
Fresh parsley, chopped (for garnish)

1. Preheat the oven to 200°C.
2. Halve the aubergines lengthwise and scoop out the flesh, leaving a 1 cm thick shell. Chop the scooped flesh and set aside.
3. Cook the quinoa according to the package instructions and set aside.
4. In a large frying pan, heat the olive oil over medium heat. Add the onion and garlic and sauté until softened, about 5 minutes.
5. Add the chopped aubergine flesh and cook for another 5 minutes.
6. Stir in the chopped tomatoes, cooked quinoa, oregano, basil, and olives. Season with salt and black pepper.
7. Stuff the aubergine shells with the quinoa mixture and place them in a baking dish.
8. Bake for 25-30 minutes, until the aubergines are tender.
9. Garnish with fresh parsley and serve hot.

Nutrition Info per Serving:

Calories: 220, Protein: 7 g, Fat: 7 g, Carbohydrates: 33 g, Fibre: 9 g, Sugar: 11 g, Sodium: 300 mg

Mushroom and Thyme Spelt

Serves: 4

|PREP TIME: 10 minutes
|COOK TIME: 30-35 minutes

2 tbsps. olive oil
200 g spelt
1 onion, finely chopped
2 garlic cloves, minced
200 g mushrooms, sliced
1 tsp. dried thyme
500 ml vegetable stock
Salt and black pepper, to taste
Fresh parsley, chopped (for garnish)

1. In a large pot over medium heat, heat the olive oil. Add the onion and garlic, and sauté until softened, about 5 minutes.
2. Stir in the sliced mushrooms and cook for another 5 minutes.
3. Add the spelt and dried thyme, and cook for 2 minutes until lightly toasted.
4. Pour in the vegetable stock and bring to a boil. Reduce the heat and simmer for 20 minutes, until the spelt is tender and the liquid is absorbed.
5. Garnish with fresh parsley and season with salt and black pepper.
6. Serve hot.

Nutrition Info per Serving:

Calories: 220, Protein: 7 g, Fat: 8 g, Carbohydrates: 30 g, Fibre: 5 g, Sugar: 3 g, Sodium: 220 mg

Grilled Aubergine Rolls

Serves: 4

2 large aubergines, thinly sliced lengthwise
2 tbsps. olive oil
100 g feta cheese, crumbled
50 g sun-dried tomatoes, chopped
1 tbsp. fresh basil, chopped
Salt and black pepper, to taste

PREP TIME: 15 minutes
COOK TIME: 10 minutes

1. Preheat the grill to medium-high heat.
2. Brush the aubergine slices with olive oil and season with salt and black pepper.
3. Grill the aubergine slices for 2-3 minutes on each side, until tender and slightly charred.
4. In a bowl, mix the feta cheese, sun-dried tomatoes, and fresh basil.
5. Place a spoonful of the feta mixture at one end of each aubergine slice and roll up.
6. Secure with a toothpick and serve.

Nutrition Info per Serving:

Calories: 100, Protein: 3 g, Fat: 8 g, Carbohydrates: 4 g, Fibre: 2 g, Sugar: 2 g, Sodium: 220 mg

Vegan Mediterranean Pizza

Serves: 4

1 ready-made pizza base
200 g tomato passata
1 tbsp. olive oil
1 yellow pepper, sliced
1 courgette, sliced
50 g black olives, sliced
1 red onion, thinly sliced
2 tbsps. nutritional yeast
1 tbsp. fresh basil, chopped
Salt and black pepper, to taste

PREP TIME: 15 minutes
COOK TIME: 15 minutes

1. Preheat the oven to 220°C.
2. Place the pizza base on a baking tray and spread the tomato passata evenly over the base.
3. Arrange the yellow pepper, courgette, black olives, and red onion on top.
4. Drizzle with olive oil and sprinkle with nutritional yeast, salt, and black pepper.
5. Bake for 12-15 minutes, until the vegetables are tender and the pizza base is crispy.
6. Garnish with fresh basil and serve hot.

Nutrition Info per Serving:

Calories: 260, Protein: 6 g, Fat: 10 g, Carbohydrates: 34 g, Fibre: 5 g, Sugar: 8 g, Sodium: 340 mg

Courgette and Tomato Gratin

Serves: 4

|PREP TIME: 10 minutes
|COOK TIME: 30 minutes

3 courgettes, sliced
4 large tomatoes, sliced
2 tbsps. olive oil
1 garlic clove, minced
50 g grated Parmesan cheese
1 tbsp. fresh thyme, chopped
Salt and black pepper, to taste

1. Preheat the oven to 180°C.
2. In a baking dish, arrange the courgette and tomato slices in an alternating pattern.
3. Drizzle with olive oil and sprinkle with minced garlic, grated Parmesan cheese, fresh thyme, salt, and black pepper.
4. Bake for 25-30 minutes, until the vegetables are tender and the cheese is golden and bubbly.
5. Serve hot.

Nutrition Info per Serving:

Calories: 150, Protein: 5 g, Fat: 10 g, Carbohydrates: 10 g, Fibre: 3 g, Sugar: 6 g, Sodium: 220 mg

Roasted Vegetable Couscous

Serves: 4

|PREP TIME: 15 minutes
|COOK TIME: 30 minutes

200 g couscous
1 red pepper, chopped
1 courgette, diced
1 red onion, chopped
2 tbsps. olive oil
1 tsp. ground cumin
1 tsp. smoked paprika
1 tsp. ground coriander
400 ml vegetable stock
Salt and black pepper, to taste
Fresh coriander, chopped (for garnish)

1. Preheat the oven to 200°C.
2. Place the red pepper, courgette, and red onion on a baking tray. Drizzle with olive oil and sprinkle with ground cumin, smoked paprika, ground coriander, salt, and black pepper. Toss to coat the vegetables evenly.
3. Roast the vegetables in the oven for 25-30 minutes, until tender and slightly charred.
4. Meanwhile, place the couscous in a large bowl. Pour over the vegetable stock, cover, and let sit for 5 minutes until the liquid is absorbed.
5. Fluff the couscous with a fork and stir in the roasted vegetables.
6. Garnish with fresh coriander and serve warm.

Nutrition Info per Serving:

Calories: 220, Protein: 6 g, Fat: 9 g, Carbohydrates: 30 g, Fibre: 5 g, Sugar: 7 g, Sodium: 300 mg

CHAPTER 3
Vegetarian and Vegan Dishes

CHAPTER 4
Fish and Seafood

Grilled Sea Bass with Lemon and Herbs ········· 22

Baked Cod with Tomatoes and Olives ········· 22

Mediterranean Tuna Steak ········· 23

Grilled Octopus with Lemon Potatoes ········· 23

Mediterranean Seafood Paella ········· 24

Garlic Prawns with Spinach ········· 24

Mussels in White Wine Sauce ········· 25

Sardines with Roasted Vegetables ········· 25

Grilled Calamari with Garlic and Lemon ········· 26

Fish Kebabs with Vegetables ········· 26

Mediterranean-style Fish Tacos ········· 27

Baked Trout with Almonds and Herbs ········· 27

Grilled Sea Bass with Lemon and Herbs

Serves: 4

PREP TIME: 10 minutes
COOK TIME: 10-15 minutes

4 sea bass fillets
2 tbsps. olive oil
1 lemon, sliced
2 garlic cloves, minced
1 tbsp. fresh parsley, chopped
1 tbsp. fresh thyme, chopped
Salt and black pepper, to taste

1. Preheat the grill to medium-high heat.
2. Brush the sea bass fillets with olive oil and season with salt and black pepper.
3. Place the lemon slices on a grill tray and lay the sea bass fillets on top.
4. Sprinkle the minced garlic, parsley, and thyme over the fish.
5. Grill for 10-15 minutes, until the fish is cooked through and flakes easily with a fork.
6. Serve hot with a squeeze of fresh lemon juice.

Nutrition Info per Serving:

Calories: 210, Protein: 25 g, Fat: 12 g, Carbohydrates: 2 g, Fibre: 1 g, Sugar: 0 g, Sodium: 150 mg

Baked Cod with Tomatoes and Olives

Serves: 4

PREP TIME: 10 minutes
COOK TIME: 30-35 minutes

4 cod fillets (about 150 g each)
2 tbsps. olive oil
1 tin of chopped tomatoes (400 g)
50 g black olives, sliced
1 red onion, finely chopped
2 garlic cloves, minced
1 tsp. dried oregano
Salt and black pepper, to taste
Fresh basil, chopped (for garnish)

1. Preheat the oven to 180°C.
2. In a large frying pan, heat 1 tbsp. of olive oil over medium heat. Add the red onion and garlic, and sauté until softened, about 5 minutes.
3. Stir in the chopped tomatoes, sliced olives, and dried oregano. Season with salt and black pepper. Simmer for 5 minutes.
4. Place the cod fillets in a baking dish and pour the tomato mixture over them.
5. Drizzle with the remaining olive oil.
6. Bake for 20-25 minutes, until the fish is cooked through and flakes easily with a fork.
7. Garnish with fresh basil and serve hot.

Nutrition Info per Serving:

Calories: 220, Protein: 28 g, Fat: 9 g, Carbohydrates: 6 g, Fibre: 2 g, Sugar: 3 g, Sodium: 250 mg

Mediterranean Tuna Steak

Serves: 2

2 tuna steaks (about 150 g each)
2 tbsps. olive oil
1 tsp. dried oregano
1 tsp. dried basil
1 lemon, juiced
1 garlic clove, minced
Salt and black pepper, to taste

PREP TIME: 10 minutes
COOK TIME: 10 minutes

1. In a small bowl, mix together the olive oil, dried oregano, dried basil, lemon juice, and minced garlic.
2. Brush the tuna steaks with the mixture and season with salt and black pepper.
3. Heat a grill pan over medium-high heat.
4. Grill the tuna steaks for 3-4 minutes on each side, until cooked to your desired level of doneness.
5. Serve hot with a drizzle of the remaining marinade.

Nutrition Info per Serving:

Calories: 260, Protein: 35 g, Fat: 12 g, Carbohydrates: 1 g, Fibre: 0 g, Sugar: 0 g, Sodium: 110 mg

Grilled Octopus with Lemon Potatoes

Serves: 4

1 kg octopus, cleaned
4 tbsps. olive oil
1 lemon, juiced
1 kg new potatoes, halved
2 garlic cloves, minced
1 tbsp. fresh parsley, chopped
Salt and black pepper, to taste

PREP TIME: 20 minutes
COOK TIME: 45 minutes

1. In a large pot, bring water to a boil and cook the octopus for 40 minutes, until tender. Drain and cut into pieces.
2. In a large frying pan, heat 2 tbsps. of olive oil over medium heat. Add the garlic and sauté for 1-2 minutes, until fragrant.
3. Add the octopus pieces and cook for 5 minutes, until slightly crispy.
4. Meanwhile, boil the new potatoes for 20-25 minutes, until tender. Drain and toss with the remaining olive oil, lemon juice, salt, and black pepper.
5. Serve the grilled octopus with the lemon potatoes and garnish with fresh parsley.

Nutrition Info per Serving:

Calories: 320, Protein: 25 g, Fat: 14 g, Carbohydrates: 24 g, Fibre: 4 g, Sugar: 2 g, Sodium: 260 mg

Mediterranean Seafood Paella

Serves: 4-6

|PREP TIME:** 15 minutes
|COOK TIME:** 40 minutes

2 tbsps. olive oil
1 onion, finely chopped
2 garlic cloves, minced
1 red pepper, chopped
200 g Arborio rice
1 tsp. smoked paprika
1 pinch of saffron threads
1 litre fish stock
200 g prawns
200 g mussels, cleaned
200 g calamari rings
1 lemon, cut into wedges
Fresh parsley, chopped (for garnish)

1. In a large pan, heat the olive oil over medium heat. Add the onion and garlic and sauté until softened, about 5 minutes.
2. Add the red pepper, and cook for another 3-5 minutes.
3. Stir in the Arborio rice, smoked paprika, and saffron threads. Cook for 2 minutes, until the rice is lightly toasted.
4. Gradually add the fish stock, one ladle at a time, stirring continuously until the liquid is absorbed before adding more.
5. After 15 minutes, add the prawns, mussels, and calamari rings. Cook for another 10 minutes, until the seafood is cooked through and the rice is tender.
6. Garnish with lemon wedges and fresh parsley.
7. Serve hot.

Nutrition Info per Serving:

Calories: 380, Protein: 25 g, Fat: 12 g, Carbohydrates: 45 g, Fibre: 3 g, Sugar: 6 g, Sodium: 360 mg

Garlic Prawns with Spinach

Serves: 2

|PREP TIME:** 10 minutes
|COOK TIME:** 10 minutes

200 g raw prawns, peeled and deveined
2 tbsps. olive oil
3 garlic cloves, minced
200 g fresh spinach
1 lemon, juiced
Salt and black pepper, to taste
Fresh parsley, chopped (for garnish)

1. In a large frying pan, heat the olive oil over medium heat. Add the garlic and sauté for 1-2 minutes, until fragrant.
2. Add the prawns and cook for 3-4 minutes, until they turn pink and are cooked through.
3. Stir in the fresh spinach and cook until wilted, about 2 minutes.
4. Drizzle with lemon juice and season with salt and black pepper.
5. Garnish with fresh parsley and serve hot.

Nutrition Info per Serving:

Calories: 220, Protein: 23 g, Fat: 12 g, Carbohydrates: 4 g, Fibre: 2 g, Sugar: 1 g, Sodium: 260 mg

CHAPTER 4
Fish and Seafood

Mussels in White Wine Sauce

Serves: 4

1 kg mussels, cleaned and debearded
2 tbsps. olive oil
1 onion, finely chopped
3 garlic cloves, minced
200 ml white wine
200 ml vegetable stock
1 tbsp. fresh parsley, chopped
Salt and black pepper, to taste

PREP TIME: 10 minutes
COOK TIME: 15 minutes

1. In a large pot, heat the olive oil over medium heat. Add the onion and garlic, and sauté until softened, about 5 minutes.
2. Add the white wine and vegetable stock, and bring to a boil.
3. Add the mussels, cover, and cook for 5-7 minutes, until the mussels have opened. Discard any mussels that do not open.
4. Season with salt and black pepper.
5. Garnish with fresh parsley and serve hot.

Nutrition Info per Serving:

Calories: 210, Protein: 18 g, Fat: 8 g, Carbohydrates: 10 g, Fibre: 1 g, Sugar: 1 g, Sodium: 320 mg

Sardines with Roasted Vegetables

Serves: 4

8 fresh sardines, cleaned
2 tbsps. olive oil
1 lemon, sliced
1 courgette, sliced
1 aubergine, sliced
1 red pepper, chopped
1 red onion, chopped
1 tsp. dried oregano
Salt and black pepper, to taste
Fresh parsley, chopped (for garnish)

PREP TIME: 10 minutes
COOK TIME: 20 minutes

1. Preheat the oven to 200°C.
2. Place the sliced courgette, aubergine, red pepper, and red onion on a baking tray. Drizzle with 1 tbsp. of olive oil and sprinkle with dried oregano, salt, and black pepper. Toss to coat.
3. Roast the vegetables in the oven for 15 minutes.
4. Meanwhile, brush the sardines with the remaining olive oil and season with salt and black pepper.
5. Place the sardines on top of the roasted vegetables and arrange the lemon slices over the sardines.
6. Return to the oven and roast for another 5 minutes, until the sardines are cooked through.
7. Garnish with fresh parsley and serve hot.

Nutrition Info per Serving:

Calories: 290, Protein: 20 g, Fat: 18 g, Carbohydrates: 10 g, Fibre: 3 g, Sugar: 4 g, Sodium: 260 mg

Grilled Calamari with Garlic and Lemon

Serves: 4

|PREP TIME: 10 minutes
|COOK TIME: 6 minutes

600 g calamari, cleaned and cut into rings
2 tbsps. olive oil
3 garlic cloves, minced
1 lemon, juiced
1 tbsp. fresh parsley, chopped
Salt and black pepper, to taste

1. Preheat the grill to medium-high heat.
2. In a bowl, toss the calamari rings with olive oil, minced garlic, lemon juice, salt, and black pepper.
3. Grill the calamari for 2-3 minutes on each side, until tender and lightly charred.
4. Garnish with fresh parsley and serve hot.

Nutrition Info per Serving:

Calories: 180, Protein: 25 g, Fat: 8 g, Carbohydrates: 2 g, Fibre: 1 g, Sugar: 0 g, Sodium: 220 mg

Fish Kebabs with Vegetables

Serves: 4

|PREP TIME: 15 minutes
|COOK TIME: 10-15 minutes

400 g white fish fillets (such as cod or haddock), cut into cubes
2 tbsps. olive oil
1 lemon, juiced
100 g cherry tomatoes
1 red pepper, chopped
1 courgette, sliced
1 tsp. dried oregano
Salt and black pepper, to taste

1. Preheat the grill to medium-high heat.
2. In a bowl, toss the fish cubes with olive oil, lemon juice, dried oregano, salt, and black pepper.
3. Thread the fish cubes and vegetables onto skewers, alternating between the fish and vegetables.
4. Grill the kebabs for 10-15 minutes, turning occasionally, until the fish is cooked through and the vegetables are tender.
5. Serve hot.

Nutrition Info per Serving:

Calories: 220, Protein: 20 g, Fat: 12 g, Carbohydrates: 8 g, Fibre: 2 g, Sugar: 3 g, Sodium: 200 mg

Mediterranean-style Fish Tacos

Serves: 4

400 g white fish fillets (such as cod or haddock)
2 tbsps. olive oil
1 tsp. smoked paprika
1 tsp. ground cumin
Salt and black pepper, to taste
8 small wholemeal tortillas
1 avocado, sliced
100 g cherry tomatoes, halved
1 red onion, thinly sliced
2 tbsps. fresh coriander, chopped
1 lime, cut into wedges

1. Preheat the oven to 180°C.
2. Place the white fish fillets on a baking tray. Drizzle with olive oil and sprinkle with smoked paprika, ground cumin, salt, and black pepper.
3. Bake for 10 minutes, until the fish is cooked through and flakes easily with a fork.
4. Meanwhile, warm the tortillas in the oven for 2-3 minutes.
5. Assemble the tacos by placing a piece of fish on each tortilla, followed by avocado slices, cherry tomatoes, red onion, and fresh coriander.
6. Serve with lime wedges.

|PREP TIME: 20 minutes
|COOK TIME: 10 minutes

Nutrition Info per Serving:

Calories: 300, Protein: 20 g, Fat: 14 g, Carbohydrates: 26 g, Fibre: 6 g, Sugar: 2 g, Sodium: 220 mg

Baked Trout with Almonds and Herbs

Serves: 4

4 trout fillets
2 tbsps. olive oil
50 g flaked almonds
1 lemon, juiced
1 tbsp. fresh parsley, chopped
1 tbsp. fresh dill, chopped
Salt and black pepper, to taste

1. Preheat the oven to 180°C.
2. Place the trout fillets in a baking dish and drizzle with olive oil.
3. Sprinkle with flaked almonds, lemon juice, parsley, and dill. Season with salt and black pepper.
4. Bake for 20-25 minutes, until the trout is cooked through and flakes easily with a fork.
5. Serve hot.

|PREP TIME: 10 minutes
|COOK TIME: 20-25 minutes

Nutrition Info per Serving:

Calories: 280, Protein: 28 g, Fat: 18 g, Carbohydrates: 4 g, Fibre: 2 g, Sugar: 1 g, Sodium: 140 mg

CHAPTER 5

Meat and Poultry

Beef and Aubergine Moussaka ··· 29

Beef and Pepper Skewers ··· 29

Beef and Tomato Stuffed Peppers ·· 30

Pork and Fennel Meatballs ··· 30

Mediterranean Pork Chops ··· 31

Pork Medallions with Balsamic Glaze ·· 31

Lamb and Spinach Curry ·· 32

Grilled Lamb and Vegetable Kebabs ·· 32

Lamb Koftas ·· 33

Chicken Souvlaki ··· 33

Herb-Roasted Turkey Breast ·· 34

Stuffed Chicken Breasts with Spinach and Feta ································· 34

Greek Lemon Chicken ··· 35

Chicken and Artichoke Stew ··· 35

Beef and Aubergine Moussaka

Serves: 4-6

2 aubergines, sliced
2 tbsps. olive oil
400 g lean beef mince
1 onion, chopped
2 garlic cloves, minced
400 g tinned chopped tomatoes
1 tsp. dried oregano
1 tsp. ground cinnamon
200 ml Greek yoghurt
50 g grated Parmesan cheese
2 eggs, beaten
Salt and black pepper, to taste

PREP TIME: 20 minutes
COOK TIME: 40 minutes

1. Preheat the oven to 180°C.
2. Brush the aubergine slices with olive oil and bake for 20 minutes until soft.
3. Meanwhile, cook the beef mince, onion, and garlic in a frying pan, until browned.
4. Add the chopped tomatoes, oregano, and cinnamon. Simmer for 10 minutes.
5. In a bowl, mix the Greek yoghurt, grated Parmesan, and beaten eggs.
6. In a baking dish, layer the aubergine slices and beef mixture. Top with the yoghurt mixture.
7. Bake for 20 minutes until golden brown.
8. Serve hot.

Nutrition Info per Serving:

Calories: 340, Protein: 28 g, Fat: 20 g, Carbohydrates: 12 g, Fibre: 4 g, Sugar: 6 g, Sodium: 400 mg

Beef and Pepper Skewers

Serves: 4

500 g sirloin steak, cut into cubes
2 red peppers, cut into chunks
2 green peppers, cut into chunks
2 tbsps. olive oil
2 tbsps. lemon juice
2 garlic cloves, minced
1 tsp. dried oregano
Salt and black pepper, to taste
Wooden skewers, soaked in water

PREP TIME: 15 minutes, plus 30 minutes for marinating
COOK TIME: 5 minutes

1. In a bowl, combine the olive oil, lemon juice, garlic, dried oregano, salt, and black pepper.
2. Add the beef cubes and toss to coat. Marinate for at least 30 minutes.
3. Preheat the grill to medium-high heat.
4. Thread the marinated beef and pepper chunks onto the skewers, alternating between the beef and peppers.
5. Grill the skewers for 2-3 minutes on each side, until the beef is cooked to your liking.
6. Serve hot.

Nutrition Info per Serving:

Calories: 250, Protein: 28 g, Fat: 14 g, Carbohydrates: 6 g, Fibre: 2 g, Sugar: 4 g, Sodium: 160 mg

Beef and Tomato Stuffed Peppers

Serves: 4

PREP TIME: 20 minutes
COOK TIME: 35-45 minutes

4 large peppers
500 g beef mince
1 onion, chopped
2 garlic cloves, minced
200 g cooked rice
400 g tinned chopped tomatoes
2 tbsps. tomato puree
1 tsp. dried oregano
1 tsp. dried basil
2 tbsps. olive oil
Salt and black pepper, to taste
Fresh parsley, chopped (for garnish)

1. Preheat the oven to 180°C.
2. Cut the tops off the peppers and remove the seeds.
3. In a large frying pan, heat the olive oil over medium heat. Add the onion and garlic, and sauté until softened, about 5 minutes.
4. Add the beef mince and cook until browned.
5. Stir in the cooked rice, chopped tomatoes, tomato puree, dried oregano, and dried basil. Season with salt and black pepper.
6. Stuff the peppers with the beef and rice mixture and place them in a baking dish.
7. Bake for 30-40 minutes, until the peppers are tender.
8. Garnish with fresh parsley and serve hot.

Nutrition Info per Serving:

Calories: 320, Protein: 24 g, Fat: 14 g, Carbohydrates: 26 g, Fibre: 5 g, Sugar: 8 g, Sodium: 300 mg

Pork and Fennel Meatballs

Serves: 4

PREP TIME: 15 minutes
COOK TIME: 20-25 minutes

500 g lean pork mince
1 fennel, finely chopped
1 onion, finely chopped
2 garlic cloves, minced
1 egg, beaten
50 g breadcrumbs
2 tbsps. fresh parsley, chopped
1 tsp. fennel seeds
Salt and black pepper, to taste
2 tbsps. olive oil

1. Preheat the oven to 180°C.
2. In a large bowl, combine the pork mince, chopped fennel, chopped onion, minced garlic, beaten egg, breadcrumbs, fresh parsley, fennel seeds, salt, and black pepper. Mix well.
3. Form the mixture into small meatballs.
4. In a large frying pan, heat the olive oil over medium heat. Brown the meatballs on all sides.
5. Transfer the meatballs to a baking dish and bake for 15 minutes, until cooked through.
6. Serve hot with your favourite sauce.

Nutrition Info per Serving:

Calories: 280, Protein: 24 g, Fat: 16 g, Carbohydrates: 10 g, Fibre: 2 g, Sugar: 3 g, Sodium: 300 mg

Mediterranean Pork Chops

Serves: 4

4 pork chops
2 tbsps. olive oil
2 garlic cloves, minced
1 tsp. dried oregano
1 tsp. dried thyme
1 lemon, sliced
Salt and black pepper, to taste

PREP TIME: 10 minutes
COOK TIME: 20 minutes

1. Preheat the oven to 180°C.
2. In a bowl, mix the olive oil, garlic, oregano, thyme, salt, and black pepper.
3. Rub the mixture onto the pork chops.
4. In an ovenproof frying pan, sear the pork chops for 2-3 minutes on each side.
5. Add the lemon slices to the pan and transfer to the oven. Bake for 15 minutes, until the pork chops are cooked through.
6. Serve hot.

Nutrition Info per Serving:

Calories: 290, Protein: 32 g, Fat: 16 g, Carbohydrates: 2 g, Fibre: 1 g, Sugar: 0 g, Sodium: 220 mg

Pork Medallions with Balsamic Glaze

Serves: 4

500 g pork tenderloin, sliced into medallions
2 tbsps. olive oil
2 garlic cloves, minced
60 ml balsamic vinegar
2 tbsps. honey
1 tsp. dried thyme
Salt and black pepper, to taste

PREP TIME: 10 minutes
COOK TIME: 20 minutes

1. In a large frying pan, heat the olive oil over medium heat. Add the pork medallions and cook for 2-3 minutes on each side until browned. Remove from the pan and set aside.
2. In the same pan, add the minced garlic and cook for 1 minute until fragrant.
3. Stir in the balsamic vinegar, honey, dried thyme, salt, and black pepper. Bring to a simmer and cook for 3-4 minutes until the sauce has thickened slightly.
4. Return the pork medallions to the pan and spoon the balsamic glaze over them. Cook for an additional 5 minutes, until the pork is cooked through and well coated with the glaze.
5. Serve hot.

Nutrition Info per Serving:

Calories: 260, Protein: 28 g, Fat: 12 g, Carbohydrates: 10 g, Fibre: 0 g, Sugar: 8 g, Sodium: 200 mg

Lamb and Spinach Curry

Serves: 4-6

|PREP TIME: 20 minutes
|COOK TIME: 40 minutes

2 tbsps. olive oil
500 g lamb shoulder, diced
1 onion, chopped
2 garlic cloves, minced
1 tsp. ground cumin
1 tsp. ground coriander
1 tsp. ground turmeric
400 g tinned chopped tomatoes
200 g fresh spinach
500 ml lamb stock
Salt and black pepper, to taste
Fresh coriander, chopped (for garnish)

1. In a large pot, heat the olive oil over medium heat. Brown the diced lamb, then remove and set aside.
2. In the same pot, cook the onion and garlic until softened.
3. Stir in the cumin, coriander, and turmeric, and cook for 1 minute.
4. Return the lamb to the pot, and add the chopped tomatoes and lamb stock. Season with salt and black pepper.
5. Bring to a boil, then reduce the heat and simmer for 30 minutes.
6. Add the fresh spinach and cook until wilted.
7. Garnish with fresh coriander and serve hot.

Nutrition Info per Serving:

Calories: 340, Protein: 28 g, Fat: 20 g, Carbohydrates: 10 g, Fibre: 3 g, Sugar: 4 g, Sodium: 400 mg

Grilled Lamb and Vegetable Kebabs

Serves: 4

|PREP TIME: 20 minutes, plus 30 minutes for marinating
|COOK TIME: 5 minutes

500 g lamb leg, cut into cubes
1 red pepper, cut into chunks
120 g mushrooms
1 courgette, sliced
2 tbsps. olive oil
2 tbsps. lemon juice
2 garlic cloves, minced
1 tsp. dried rosemary
Salt and black pepper, to taste
Wooden skewers, soaked in water

1. In a bowl, combine the olive oil, lemon juice, garlic, dried rosemary, salt, and black pepper.
2. Add the lamb cubes and toss to coat. Marinate for at least 30 minutes.
3. Preheat the grill to medium-high heat.
4. Thread the marinated lamb, pepper chunks, mushrooms and courgette slices onto the skewers, alternating between the lamb and vegetables.
5. Grill the skewers for 2-3 minutes on each side, until the lamb is cooked to your liking.
6. Serve hot.

Nutrition Info per Serving:

Calories: 260, Protein: 26 g, Fat: 16 g, Carbohydrates: 6 g, Fibre: 2 g, Sugar: 3 g, Sodium: 200 mg

CHAPTER 5
Meat and Poultry

Lamb Koftas

Serves: 4

400 g lamb mince
1 onion, finely chopped
2 garlic cloves, minced
2 tbsps. fresh parsley, chopped
1 tbsp. ground cumin
1 tbsp. ground coriander
1 tsp. ground cinnamon
Salt and black pepper, to taste
1 tbsp. olive oil

|PREP TIME: 20 minutes
|COOK TIME: 15 minutes

1. In a bowl, combine the lamb mince, onion, garlic, parsley, cumin, coriander, cinnamon, salt, and black pepper. Mix well.
2. Shape the mixture into small kebabs.
3. In a frying pan, heat the olive oil over medium heat. Cook the kebabs for 7-8 minutes on each side, until cooked through.
4. Serve hot with a side of yoghurt sauce.

Nutrition Info per Serving:

Calories: 320, Protein: 25 g, Fat: 22 g, Carbohydrates: 4 g, Fibre: 1 g, Sugar: 1 g, Sodium: 200 mg

Chicken Souvlaki

Serves: 4

500 g chicken breast, cut into cubes
2 tbsps. olive oil
2 tbsps. lemon juice
2 garlic cloves, minced
1 tsp. dried oregano
Salt and black pepper, to taste
Wooden skewers, soaked in water

|PREP TIME: 20 minutes, plus 30 minutes marinating
|COOK TIME: 8 minutes

1. In a bowl, combine the olive oil, lemon juice, garlic, dried oregano, salt, and black pepper.
2. Add the chicken cubes and toss to coat. Marinate for at least 30 minutes.
3. Preheat the grill to medium-high heat.
4. Thread the marinated chicken onto the skewers.
5. Grill the skewers for 3-4 minutes on each side, until the chicken is cooked through.
6. Serve hot with a side of tzatziki sauce.

Nutrition Info per Serving:

Calories: 180, Protein: 28 g, Fat: 7 g, Carbohydrates: 1 g, Fibre: 0 g, Sugar: 0 g, Sodium: 160 mg

Herb-Roasted Turkey Breast

Serves: 2-4

PREP TIME: 15 minutes
COOK TIME: 1 hour

500 g turkey breast
2 tbsps. olive oil
1 tbsp. fresh rosemary, chopped
1 tbsp. fresh thyme, chopped
2 garlic cloves, minced
Zest of 1 lemon
Salt and black pepper, to taste

1. Preheat the oven to 180°C.
2. In a small bowl, combine the olive oil, rosemary, thyme, garlic, lemon zest, salt, and black pepper.
3. Rub the mixture all over the turkey breast.
4. Place the turkey in a roasting pan and roast for 1 hour, or until the internal temperature reaches 75°C.
5. Allow the turkey to rest for 10 minutes before slicing.
6. Serve hot.

Nutrition Info per Serving:

Calories: 200, Protein: 34 g, Fat: 7 g, Carbohydrates: 1 g, Fibre: 0 g, Sugar: 0 g, Sodium: 180 mg

Stuffed Chicken Breasts with Spinach and Feta

Serves: 4

PREP TIME: 20 minutes
COOK TIME: 25 minutes

4 chicken breasts
100 g spinach, chopped
100 g feta cheese, crumbled
2 garlic cloves, minced
2 tbsps. olive oil
1 tsp. dried oregano
Salt and black pepper, to taste

1. Preheat the oven to 180°C.
2. In a bowl, combine the chopped spinach, feta cheese, minced garlic, olive oil, dried oregano, salt, and black pepper.
3. Cut a slit in each chicken breast to create a pocket. Stuff each pocket with the spinach and feta mixture.
4. Place the stuffed chicken breasts in a baking dish and drizzle with a little more olive oil.
5. Bake for 25 minutes, until the chicken is cooked through.
6. Serve hot.

Nutrition Info per Serving:

Calories: 250, Protein: 34 g, Fat: 12 g, Carbohydrates: 2 g, Fibre: 0 g, Sugar: 0 g, Sodium: 300 mg

CHAPTER 5
Meat and Poultry

Greek Lemon Chicken

Serves: 4

500 g chicken thighs, bone-in and skinless
2 tbsps. olive oil
3 garlic cloves, minced
Zest and juice of 2 lemons
1 tbsp. dried oregano
1 tsp. dried thyme
1 tsp. paprika
Salt and black pepper, to taste
Fresh parsley, chopped (for garnish)

PREP TIME: 10 minutes
COOK TIME: 45 minutes

1. Preheat the oven to 200°C.
2. In a bowl, combine the olive oil, garlic, lemon zest, lemon juice, dried oregano, dried thyme, paprika, salt, and black pepper.
3. Add the chicken thighs and toss to coat.
4. Place the chicken thighs in a baking dish and pour any remaining marinade over them.
5. Bake for 45 minutes, until the chicken is cooked through and golden brown.
6. Garnish with fresh parsley and serve hot.

Nutrition Info per Serving:

Calories: 250, Protein: 26 g, Fat: 14 g, Carbohydrates: 3 g, Fibre: 1 g, Sugar: 1 g, Sodium: 300 mg

Chicken and Artichoke Stew

Serves: 4

500 g chicken breast, cut into chunks
2 tbsps. olive oil
1 onion, chopped
2 garlic cloves, minced
400 g tinned artichoke hearts, drained and halved
400 g tinned chopped tomatoes
200 ml chicken stock
1 tsp. dried oregano
1 tsp. dried thyme
Salt and black pepper, to taste

PREP TIME: 15 minutes
COOK TIME: 50 minutes

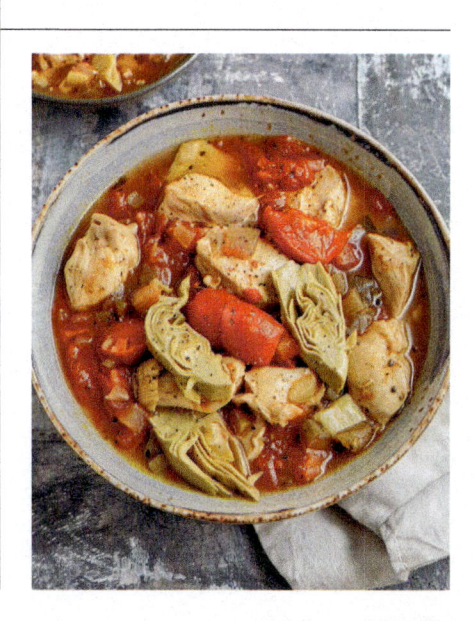

1. In a large pot, heat the olive oil over medium heat. Add the onion and garlic, and sauté until softened, about 5 minutes.
2. Add the chicken chunks and cook until browned on all sides.
3. Stir in the artichoke hearts, chopped tomatoes, chicken stock, dried oregano, and dried thyme. Season with salt and black pepper.
4. Bring to a boil, then reduce the heat and simmer for 45 minutes, until the chicken is tender and the flavours have melded.
5. Serve hot.

Nutrition Info per Serving:

Calories: 230, Protein: 28 g, Fat: 10 g, Carbohydrates: 8 g, Fibre: 3 g, Sugar: 4 g, Sodium: 400 mg

CHAPTER 6
Pasta and Salads

Rocket and Parmesan Salad ··· 37

Quinoa and Avocado Salad ··· 37

Mediterranean Penne with Sun-dried Tomatoes ················· 38

Spinach and Ricotta Cannelloni ·· 38

Vegan Pesto Pasta ··· 39

Seafood Linguine with Cherry Tomatoes ····························· 39

Pesto Pasta with Roasted Vegetables ·································· 40

Spaghetti with Lemon and Capers ·· 40

Roasted Red Pepper and Olive Salad ··································· 41

Caprese Salad ·· 41

Artichoke and Sun-dried Tomato Salad ································ 42

Tabbouleh Salad ·· 42

Rocket and Parmesan Salad

Serves: 4

200 g rocket leaves
50 g Parmesan cheese, shaved
2 tbsps. olive oil
1 tbsp. balsamic vinegar
Salt and black pepper, to taste

|PREP TIME: 5 minutes
|COOK TIME: 0 minutes

1. In a large bowl, combine the rocket leaves and shaved Parmesan cheese.
2. Drizzle with olive oil and balsamic vinegar. Toss to combine.
3. Season with salt and black pepper.
4. Serve immediately.

Nutrition Info per Serving:

Calories: 160, Protein: 6 g, Fat: 14 g, Carbohydrates: 2 g, Fibre: 1 g, Sugar: 1 g, Sodium: 220 mg

Quinoa and Avocado Salad

Serves: 4

200 g quinoa
1 avocado, diced
1 cucumber, diced
1 red pepper, diced
100 g cherry tomatoes, halved
2 tbsps. olive oil
1 tbsp. lemon juice
1 tbsp. fresh coriander, chopped
Salt and black pepper, to taste

|PREP TIME: 10 minutes
|COOK TIME: 15 minutes

1. Cook the quinoa according to the package instructions. Drain and set aside to cool.
2. In a large bowl, combine the cooled quinoa, diced avocado, cucumber, red pepper, and cherry tomatoes.
3. Drizzle with olive oil and lemon juice. Toss to combine.
4. Season with salt and black pepper.
5. Garnish with fresh coriander and serve immediately.

Nutrition Info per Serving:

Calories: 240, Protein: 6 g, Fat: 12 g, Carbohydrates: 26 g, Fibre: 7 g, Sugar: 3 g, Sodium: 180 mg

Mediterranean Penne with Sun-dried Tomatoes

Serves: 4

|PREP TIME: 10 minutes
|COOK TIME: 15 minutes

300 g penne pasta
2 tbsps. olive oil
3 garlic cloves, minced
100 g sun-dried tomatoes, chopped
1 red pepper, chopped
50 g black olives, sliced
2 tbsps. fresh basil, chopped
Salt and black pepper, to taste
Grated Parmesan cheese (optional)

1. Cook the penne pasta according to the package instructions. Drain and set aside.
2. In a large frying pan, heat the olive oil over medium heat. Add the garlic and sauté for 1-2 minutes until fragrant.
3. Add the sun-dried tomatoes, red pepper, and black olives. Cook for 5 minutes, stirring occasionally.
4. Add the cooked pasta to the pan and toss to combine.
5. Season with salt and black pepper.
6. Garnish with fresh basil and grated Parmesan cheese, if desired.
7. Serve hot.

Nutrition Info per Serving:

Calories: 320, Protein: 9 g, Fat: 10 g, Carbohydrates: 50 g, Fibre: 4 g, Sugar: 7 g, Sodium: 250 mg

Spinach and Ricotta Cannelloni

Serves: 4

|PREP TIME: 15 minutes
|COOK TIME: 40 minutes

200 g cannelloni tubes
250 g ricotta cheese
200 g fresh spinach, chopped
1 egg, beaten
50 g grated Parmesan cheese
1 tin of chopped tomatoes (400 g)
1 onion, finely chopped
2 garlic cloves, minced
2 tbsps. olive oil
Salt and black pepper, to taste
Fresh basil, chopped (for garnish)

1. Preheat the oven to 180°C.
2. In a bowl, mix the ricotta cheese, chopped spinach, beaten egg, and half of the grated Parmesan cheese. Season with salt and black pepper.
3. Fill the cannelloni tubes with the ricotta mixture and place them in a baking dish.
4. In a frying pan, heat the olive oil over medium heat. Add the onion and garlic, and sauté until softened, about 5 minutes.
5. Stir in the chopped tomatoes and cook for another 5 minutes. Season with salt and black pepper.
6. Pour the tomato sauce over the cannelloni and sprinkle with the remaining Parmesan cheese.
7. Bake for 25-30 minutes, until the cheese is golden and bubbly.
8. Garnish with fresh basil and serve hot.

Nutrition Info per Serving:

Calories: 350, Protein: 15 g, Fat: 16 g, Carbohydrates: 38 g, Fibre: 5 g, Sugar: 8 g, Sodium: 320 mg

CHAPTER 6
Pasta and Salads

Vegan Pesto Pasta

Serves: 4

300 g wholemeal pasta
50 g fresh basil leaves
30 g pine nuts
1 garlic clove
2 tbsps. nutritional yeast
60 ml olive oil
1 tbsp. lemon juice
Salt and black pepper, to taste
200 g cherry tomatoes, halved

|PREP TIME: 10 minutes
|COOK TIME: 10 minutes

1. Cook the pasta according to the package instructions. Drain and set aside.
2. In a food processor, combine the basil leaves, pine nuts, garlic, nutritional yeast, olive oil, and lemon juice. Blend until smooth. Season with salt and black pepper to taste.
3. In a large bowl, toss the cooked pasta with the pesto sauce and cherry tomatoes.
4. Serve immediately.

Nutrition Info per Serving:

Calories: 350, Protein: 10 g, Fat: 18 g, Carbohydrates: 38 g, Fibre: 6 g, Sugar: 4 g, Sodium: 120 mg

Seafood Linguine with Cherry Tomatoes

Serves: 4

300 g wholemeal linguine pasta
2 tbsps. olive oil
3 garlic cloves, minced
200 g cherry tomatoes, halved
200 g mixed seafood (such as prawns, calamari, and mussels)
1 lemon, juiced
2 tbsps. fresh parsley, chopped
Salt and black pepper, to taste

|PREP TIME: 10 minutes
|COOK TIME: 20 minutes

1. Cook the linguine pasta according to the package instructions. Drain and set aside.
2. In a large frying pan, heat the olive oil over medium heat. Add the garlic and sauté for 1-2 minutes until fragrant.
3. Add the cherry tomatoes and cook for 3-4 minutes until they start to soften.
4. Add the mixed seafood and cook for another 5 minutes until the seafood is cooked through.
5. Stir in the cooked linguine, lemon juice, and fresh parsley. Toss to combine.
6. Season with salt and black pepper.
7. Serve hot.

Nutrition Info per Serving:

Calories: 340, Protein: 18 g, Fat: 10 g, Carbohydrates: 46 g, Fibre: 3 g, Sugar: 6 g, Sodium: 320 mg

Pesto Pasta with Roasted Vegetables

Serves: 4

PREP TIME: 15 minutes
COOK TIME: 25 minutes

300 g wholemeal pasta
2 courgettes, sliced
1 red pepper, chopped
1 yellow pepper, chopped
1 red onion, chopped
2 tbsps. olive oil
100 g pesto (store-bought or homemade)
2 tbsps. pine nuts, toasted
Salt and black pepper, to taste

1. Preheat the oven to 200°C.
2. Place the courgettes, red pepper, yellow pepper, and red onion on a baking tray. Drizzle with olive oil, season with salt and black pepper, and toss to coat.
3. Roast the vegetables for 20-25 minutes, until tender and slightly charred.
4. Meanwhile, cook the pasta according to the package instructions. Drain and set aside.
5. In a large bowl, combine the cooked pasta, roasted vegetables, and pesto. Toss to coat evenly.
6. Garnish with toasted pine nuts and serve hot.

Nutrition Info per Serving:

Calories: 320, Protein: 9 g, Fat: 14 g, Carbohydrates: 40 g, Fibre: 7 g, Sugar: 8 g, Sodium: 200 mg

Spaghetti with Lemon and Capers

Serves: 4

PREP TIME: 10 minutes
COOK TIME: 15 minutes

300 g spaghetti
2 tbsps. olive oil
3 garlic cloves, minced
2 tbsps. capers, rinsed
1 lemon, juiced and zested
2 tbsps. fresh parsley, chopped
Salt and black pepper, to taste

1. Cook the spaghetti according to the package instructions. Drain and set aside.
2. In a large frying pan, heat the olive oil over medium heat. Add the garlic and sauté for 1-2 minutes until fragrant.
3. Add the capers and cook for another 2 minutes.
4. Stir in the cooked spaghetti, lemon juice, and lemon zest. Toss to combine.
5. Season with salt and black pepper.
6. Garnish with fresh parsley and serve hot.

Nutrition Info per Serving:

Calories: 280, Protein: 7 g, Fat: 10 g, Carbohydrates: 42 g, Fibre: 4 g, Sugar: 2 g, Sodium: 180 mg

CHAPTER 6
Pasta and Salads

Roasted Red Pepper and Olive Salad

Serves: 4

4 red peppers
100 g black olives, sliced
1 red onion, thinly sliced
2 tbsps. olive oil
1 tbsp. red wine vinegar
1 tbsp. fresh basil, chopped
Salt and black pepper, to taste

PREP TIME: 10 minutes
COOK TIME: 20 minutes

1. Preheat the oven to 200°C.
2. Place the red peppers on a baking tray and roast for 20 minutes, until the skins are charred.
3. Remove from the oven, place in a bowl, and cover with cling film. Let them cool, then peel and slice the peppers.
4. In a large bowl, combine the sliced peppers, black olives, and red onion.
5. Drizzle with olive oil and red wine vinegar. Toss to combine.
6. Garnish with fresh basil and season with salt and black pepper.
7. Serve immediately.

Nutrition Info per Serving:

Calories: 150, Protein: 2 g, Fat: 12 g, Carbohydrates: 10 g, Fibre: 3 g, Sugar: 5 g, Sodium: 220 mg

Caprese Salad

Serves: 4

3 large tomatoes, sliced
250 g fresh mozzarella cheese, sliced
1 bunch of fresh basil leaves
2 tbsps. olive oil
1 tbsp. balsamic vinegar
Salt and black pepper, to taste

PREP TIME: 10 minutes
COOK TIME: 0 minutes

1. Arrange the tomato and mozzarella slices on a serving platter, alternating between them.
2. Tuck the fresh basil leaves between the tomato and mozzarella slices.
3. Drizzle with olive oil and balsamic vinegar.
4. Season with salt and black pepper.
5. Serve immediately.

Nutrition Info per Serving:

Calories: 250, Protein: 12 g, Fat: 20 g, Carbohydrates: 6 g, Fibre: 2 g, Sugar: 4 g, Sodium: 280 mg

CHAPTER 6
Pasta and Salads

Artichoke and Sun-dried Tomato Salad

Serves: 4

PREP TIME: 10 minutes
COOK TIME: 0 minutes

200 g artichoke hearts, drained and chopped
100 g sun-dried tomatoes, chopped
50 g black olives, sliced
1 red onion, thinly sliced
2 tbsps. olive oil
1 tbsp. lemon juice
1 tbsp. fresh parsley, chopped
Salt and black pepper, to taste

1. In a large bowl, combine the artichoke hearts, sun-dried tomatoes, black olives, and red onion.
2. Drizzle with olive oil and lemon juice. Toss to combine.
3. Garnish with fresh parsley and season with salt and black pepper.
4. Serve immediately.

Nutrition Info per Serving:

Calories: 180, Protein: 3 g, Fat: 12 g, Carbohydrates: 14 g, Fibre: 6 g, Sugar: 5 g, Sodium: 260 mg

Tabbouleh Salad

Serves: 4

PREP TIME: 15 minutes
COOK TIME: 15 minutes

200 g bulgur wheat
1 bunch of fresh parsley, chopped
1 bunch of fresh mint, chopped
2 large tomatoes, diced
1 cucumber, diced
1 red onion, finely chopped
3 tbsps. olive oil
2 tbsps. lemon juice
Salt and black pepper, to taste

1. Cook the bulgur wheat according to the package instructions. Drain and set aside to cool.
2. In a large bowl, combine the cooled bulgur wheat, chopped parsley, mint, tomatoes, cucumber, and red onion.
3. Drizzle with olive oil and lemon juice.
4. Toss to combine and season with salt and black pepper.
5. Serve immediately.

Nutrition Info per Serving:

Calories: 220, Protein: 5 g, Fat: 10 g, Carbohydrates: 28 g, Fibre: 6 g, Sugar: 4 g, Sodium: 180 mg

CHAPTER 6
Pasta and Salads

CHAPTER 7
Soups and Stews

Spiced Carrot and Lentil Soup ··· 44

Artichoke and Potato Stew ··· 44

Spanish Gazpacho ··· 45

Fennel and Leek Soup ··· 45

Greek Lemon Chicken Soup ··· 46

Chickpea and Spinach Stew ··· 46

Italian Minestrone ··· 47

Tomato and Basil Soup ··· 47

Seafood Cioppino ··· 48

Aubergine and Tomato Stew ··· 48

Pumpkin and Red Pepper Soup ··· 49

White Bean and Spinach Soup ··· 49

Spiced Carrot and Lentil Soup

Serves: 4

|PREP TIME:** 10 minutes
|COOK TIME:** 30 minutes

2 tbsps. olive oil
4 carrots, chopped
200 g red lentils
1 litre vegetable stock
1 onion, chopped
2 garlic cloves, minced
1 tsp. ground cumin
1 tsp. ground coriander
1 tsp. ground turmeric
Salt and black pepper, to taste
Fresh coriander, chopped (for garnish)

1. In a large pot, heat the olive oil over medium heat. Add the onion and garlic, and sauté until softened, about 5 minutes.
2. Add the chopped carrots and cook for another 5 minutes.
3. Stir in the red lentils, vegetable stock, ground cumin, ground coriander, and ground turmeric. Season with salt and black pepper.
4. Bring to a boil, then reduce the heat and simmer for 20 minutes, until the lentils and carrots are tender.
5. Blend the soup until smooth using an immersion blender or a regular blender.
6. Garnish with fresh coriander and serve hot.

Nutrition Info per Serving:

Calories: 200, Protein: 9 g, Fat: 8 g, Carbohydrates: 26 g, Fibre: 8 g, Sugar: 7 g, Sodium: 260 mg

Artichoke and Potato Stew

Serves: 4

|PREP TIME:** 10 minutes
|COOK TIME:** 30 minutes

2 tbsps. olive oil
4 potatoes, peeled and diced
200 g artichoke hearts, drained and chopped
400 g tinned chopped tomatoes
1 litre vegetable stock
1 onion, chopped
2 garlic cloves, minced
1 tsp. dried thyme
1 tsp. dried rosemary
Salt and black pepper, to taste
Fresh parsley, chopped (for garnish)

1. In a large pot, heat the olive oil over medium heat. Add the onion and garlic, and sauté until softened, about 5 minutes.
2. Add the diced potatoes and cook for another 5 minutes.
3. Stir in the artichoke hearts, chopped tomatoes, vegetable stock, dried thyme, and dried rosemary. Season with salt and black pepper.
4. Bring to a boil, then reduce the heat and simmer for 20 minutes, until the potatoes are tender.
5. Garnish with fresh parsley and serve hot.

Nutrition Info per Serving:

Calories: 200, Protein: 5 g, Fat: 10 g, Carbohydrates: 24 g, Fibre: 6 g, Sugar: 6 g, Sodium: 240 mg

CHAPTER 7
Soups and Stews

Spanish Gazpacho

Serves: 4

4 large tomatoes, chopped
1 cucumber, peeled and chopped
1 red pepper, chopped
1 green pepper, chopped
1 red onion, chopped
2 garlic cloves, minced
3 tbsps. olive oil
2 tbsps. red wine vinegar
1 slice of wholemeal bread, soaked in water and squeezed dry
Salt and black pepper, to taste
Fresh basil, chopped (for garnish)

PREP TIME: 15 minutes
COOK TIME: 0 minutes

1. In a blender, combine the tomatoes, cucumber, red pepper, green pepper, red onion, garlic, olive oil, red wine vinegar, and soaked bread.
2. Blend until smooth. Season with salt and black pepper.
3. Chill in the refrigerator for at least 2 hours before serving.
4. Garnish with fresh basil and serve cold.

Nutrition Info per Serving:

Calories: 160, Protein: 3 g, Fat: 10 g, Carbohydrates: 16 g, Fibre: 4 g, Sugar: 7 g, Sodium: 220 mg

Fennel and Leek Soup

Serves: 4

2 tbsps. olive oil
2 leeks, sliced
1 fennel, sliced
2 garlic cloves, minced
1 litre vegetable stock
200 g potatoes, peeled and diced
1 tsp. dried thyme
Salt and black pepper, to taste
Fresh dill, chopped (for garnish)

PREP TIME: 10 minutes
COOK TIME: 25 minutes

1. In a large frying pan, heat the olive oil over medium heat. Add the sliced leeks, fennel, and garlic, and sauté until softened, about 5 minutes.
2. Stir in the vegetable stock, diced potatoes, and dried thyme. Season with salt and black pepper.
3. Bring to a boil, then reduce the heat and simmer for about 20 minutes, until the vegetables are tender.
4. Blend the soup until smooth using an immersion blender or a regular blender.
5. Garnish with fresh dill and serve hot.

Nutrition Info per Serving:

Calories: 170, Protein: 3 g, Fat: 10 g, Carbohydrates: 18 g, Fibre: 4 g, Sugar: 6 g, Sodium: 200 mg

Greek Lemon Chicken Soup

Serves: 4

PREP TIME: 10 minutes
COOK TIME: 25 minutes

1 tbsp. olive oil
200 g cooked chicken, shredded
100 g orzo pasta
100 g celery stick, chopped
100 g carrot, chopped
60 g onion, chopped
2 eggs
2 lemons, juiced
2 garlic cloves, minced
1 litre chicken stock
Salt and black pepper, to taste
Fresh dill, chopped (for garnish)

1. In a pot, heat the olive oil over medium heat. Add the onion and garlic, and sauté until softened, about 5 minutes.
2. Add the carrot and celery, and cook for another 5 minutes.
3. Stir in the chicken stock, shredded chicken, and orzo pasta. Bring to a boil, then reduce the heat and simmer for 15 minutes, until the pasta is cooked.
4. In a small bowl, whisk together the eggs and lemon juice.
5. Gradually ladle some hot soup into the egg mixture, whisking constantly to temper the eggs.
6. Slowly stir the egg mixture back into the pot, and cook for another 2 minutes, until the soup is slightly thickened.
7. Season with salt and black pepper.
8. Garnish with fresh dill and serve hot.

Nutrition Info per Serving:

Calories: 220, Protein: 16 g, Fat: 9 g, Carbohydrates: 18 g, Fibre: 2 g, Sugar: 3 g, Sodium: 300 mg

Chickpea and Spinach Stew

Serves: 4

PREP TIME: 10 minutes
COOK TIME: 25 minutes

2 tbsps. olive oil
1 tin of chickpeas (400 g), drained and rinsed
400 g tinned chopped tomatoes
200 g fresh spinach
50 g onion, chopped
2 garlic cloves, minced
1 tsp. ground cumin
1 tsp. ground coriander
Salt and black pepper, to taste
Fresh coriander, chopped (for garnish)

1. In a large pot, heat the olive oil over medium-high heat. Add the onion and garlic, and sauté until softened, about 3-5 minutes.
2. Stir in the chickpeas, chopped tomatoes, ground cumin, and ground coriander. Season with salt and black pepper.
3. Bring to a boil, then reduce the heat and simmer for 15 minutes.
4. Add the fresh spinach and cook until wilted, about 2 minutes.
5. Garnish with fresh coriander and serve hot.

Nutrition Info per Serving:

Calories: 180, Protein: 7 g, Fat: 7 g, Carbohydrates: 24 g, Fibre: 8 g, Sugar: 7 g, Sodium: 260 mg

Italian Minestrone

Serves: 4

2 tbsps. olive oil
1 tin of chopped tomatoes (400 g)
400 g tinned cannellini beans, drained and rinsed
100 g pasta (small shapes)
2 celery sticks, chopped
2 carrots, chopped
1 courgette, chopped
1 onion, chopped
2 garlic cloves, minced
1 litre vegetable stock
1 tsp. dried oregano
1 tsp. dried basil
Salt and black pepper, to taste
Fresh basil, chopped (for garnish)

PREP TIME: 15 minutes
COOK TIME: 30 minutes

1. In a large pot, heat the olive oil over medium heat. Add the onion and garlic, and sauté until softened, about 5 minutes.
2. Add the carrots, celery, and courgette, and cook for another 5 minutes.
3. Stir in the chopped tomatoes, cannellini beans, vegetable stock, pasta, dried oregano, and dried basil. Season with salt and black pepper.
4. Bring to a boil, then reduce the heat and simmer for 20 minutes, until the pasta and vegetables are tender.
5. Garnish with fresh basil and serve hot.

Nutrition Info per Serving:

Calories: 230, Protein: 8 g, Fat: 8 g, Carbohydrates: 34 g, Fibre: 8 g, Sugar: 8 g, Sodium: 280 mg

Tomato and Basil Soup

Serves: 4

2 tbsps. olive oil
800 g tinned chopped tomatoes
500 ml vegetable stock
1 onion, chopped
2 garlic cloves, minced
1 tsp. dried oregano
Salt and black pepper, to taste
Fresh basil, chopped (for garnish)

PREP TIME: 10 minutes
COOK TIME: 25 minutes

1. In a large pot, heat the olive oil over medium-high heat. Add the onion and garlic, and sauté until softened, about 3-5 minutes.
2. Stir in the chopped tomatoes, vegetable stock, and dried oregano. Season with salt and black pepper.
3. Bring to a boil, then reduce the heat and simmer for 20 minutes.
4. Blend the soup until smooth using an immersion blender or a regular blender.
5. Garnish with fresh basil and serve hot.

Nutrition Info per Serving:

Calories: 150, Protein: 4 g, Fat: 7 g, Carbohydrates: 18 g, Fibre: 5 g, Sugar: 10 g, Sodium: 260 mg

Seafood Cioppino

Serves: 4

|PREP TIME: 15 minutes
|COOK TIME: 40 minutes

2 tbsps. olive oil
200 g cod fillets, cubed
200 g prawns
200 g mussels, cleaned
1 onion, chopped
1 fennel, sliced
500 ml fish stock
400 g tinned chopped tomatoes
200 ml white wine
2 garlic cloves, minced
1 tsp. dried thyme
1 tsp. dried oregano
Salt and black pepper, to taste
Fresh parsley, chopped (for garnish)

1. In a large pot, heat the olive oil over medium heat. Add the onion and garlic, and sauté until softened, about 3-5 minutes.
2. Add the red pepper and yellow pepper, and cook for another 5 minutes.
3. Stir in the chopped tomatoes, fish stock, dried thyme, and dried basil. Season with salt and black pepper.
4. Bring to a boil, then reduce the heat and simmer for 20 minutes.
5. Add the cod and haddock, and simmer for another 10 minutes, until the fish is cooked through.
6. Garnish with fresh parsley and serve hot.

Nutrition Info per Serving:

Calories: 230, Protein: 28 g, Fat: 8 g, Carbohydrates: 10 g, Fibre: 2 g, Sugar: 4 g, Sodium: 280 mg

Aubergine and Tomato Stew

Serves: 4

|PREP TIME: 10 minutes
|COOK TIME: 25 minutes

2 tbsps. olive oil
400 g tinned chopped tomatoes
1 large aubergine, diced
1 red pepper, chopped
1 yellow pepper, chopped
1 onion, chopped
2 garlic cloves, minced
1 tsp. ground cumin
1 tsp. ground coriander
1 tsp. dried oregano
Salt and black pepper, to taste
Fresh parsley, chopped (for garnish)

1. In a large pan over medium heat, heat the olive oil. Add the onion and garlic, and cook until softened, about 5 minutes.
2. Add the diced aubergine and cook for another 5 minutes.
3. Stir in the chopped tomatoes, red pepper, yellow pepper, ground cumin, ground coriander, and dried oregano. Season with salt and black pepper.
4. Bring to a boil, then reduce the heat and simmer for 20 minutes, until the vegetables are tender.
5. Garnish with fresh parsley and serve hot.

Nutrition Info per Serving:

Calories: 180, Protein: 4 g, Fat: 10 g, Carbohydrates: 20 g, Fibre: 7 g, Sugar: 10 g, Sodium: 220 mg

Pumpkin and Red Pepper Soup

Serves: 4

2 tbsps. olive oil
500 g pumpkin, peeled and diced
400 g tinned chopped tomatoes
1 litre vegetable stock
1 red pepper, chopped
1 onion, chopped
2 garlic cloves, minced
1 tsp. ground cumin
1 tsp. ground coriander
Salt and black pepper, to taste
Fresh coriander, chopped (for garnish)

PREP TIME: 10 minutes
COOK TIME: 30 minutes

1. In a large pot, heat the olive oil over medium-high heat. Add the onion and garlic, and sauté until softened, about 3-5 minutes.
2. Add the diced pumpkin and red pepper, and cook for another 5 minutes.
3. Stir in the chopped tomatoes, vegetable stock, ground cumin, and ground coriander. Season with salt and black pepper.
4. Bring to a boil, then reduce the heat and simmer for 20 minutes, until the pumpkin is tender.
5. Blend the soup until smooth using an immersion blender or a regular blender.
6. Garnish with fresh coriander and serve hot.

Nutrition Info per Serving:

Calories: 190, Protein: 4 g, Fat: 10 g, Carbohydrates: 22 g, Fibre: 6 g, Sugar: 10 g, Sodium: 240 mg

White Bean and Spinach Soup

Serves: 4

2 tbsps. olive oil
2 carrots, chopped
200 g fresh spinach
1 onion, chopped
400 g tinned cannellini beans, drained and rinsed
1 litre vegetable stock
2 garlic cloves, minced
1 tsp. dried thyme
Salt and black pepper, to taste
Fresh parsley, chopped (for garnish)

PREP TIME: 10 minutes
COOK TIME: 25-30 minutes

1. In a large pot, heat the olive oil over medium heat. Add the onion and garlic, and sauté until softened, about 5 minutes.
2. Add the chopped carrots and cook for another 5 minutes.
3. Stir in the cannellini beans, vegetable stock, and dried thyme. Season with salt and black pepper.
4. Bring to a boil, then reduce the heat and simmer for 15 minutes.
5. Add the fresh spinach and cook until wilted, about 2 minutes.
6. Garnish with fresh parsley and serve hot.

Nutrition Info per Serving:

Calories: 180, Protein: 7 g, Fat: 8 g, Carbohydrates: 22 g, Fibre: 7 g, Sugar: 5 g, Sodium: 260 mg

CHAPTER 8
Beans and Grains

Mediterranean Black Bean Tacos ·················· 51

Lentil and Vegetable Shepherd's Pie ·················· 51

Baked Falafel with Tahini Sauce ·················· 52

Lemon and Herb Couscous ·················· 52

Greek Gigantes Beans ·················· 53

Prawn and Asparagus Risotto ·················· 53

Lentil and Mushroom Stuffed Cabbage Rolls ·················· 54

Tomato and Basil Barley ·················· 54

Spiced Rice with Chickpeas ·················· 55

Moroccan Spiced Lentils ·················· 55

Roasted Vegetable Bulgur ·················· 56

Pea and Mint Orzo ·················· 56

Mediterranean Black Bean Tacos

Serves: 4

1 tin of black beans (400 g), drained and rinsed
1 red pepper, diced
1 yellow pepper, diced
1 red onion, finely chopped
2 garlic cloves, minced
2 tbsps. olive oil
1 tsp. ground cumin
1 tsp. smoked paprika
Salt and black pepper, to taste
8 small wholemeal tortillas
Fresh coriander, chopped (for garnish)
1 lime, cut into wedges

PREP TIME: 10 minutes
COOK TIME: 15 minutes

1. In a frying pan, heat the olive oil over medium heat. Add the onion and garlic, and sauté until softened, about 5 minutes.
2. Stir in the red pepper, yellow pepper, ground cumin, and smoked paprika. Cook for another 5 minutes, until the peppers are tender.
3. Add the black beans and cook for another 2-3 minutes, until heated through. Season with salt and black pepper.
4. Warm the tortillas in a separate pan or oven.
5. Spoon the black bean mixture onto the tortillas and garnish with fresh coriander.
6. Serve with lime wedges.

Nutrition Info per Serving:

Calories: 240, Protein: 9 g, Fat: 10 g, Carbohydrates: 30 g, Fibre: 6 g, Sugar: 3 g, Sodium: 200 mg

Lentil and Vegetable Shepherd's Pie

Serves: 4

200 g red lentils, rinsed
2 tbsps. olive oil
1 onion, chopped
2 garlic cloves, minced
2 carrots, diced
1 courgette, diced
200 g tinned chopped tomatoes
1 tsp. dried thyme
1 tsp. dried rosemary
Salt and black pepper, to taste
500 g potatoes, peeled and chopped
50 g grated Cheddar cheese

PREP TIME: 20 minutes
COOK TIME: 50 minutes

1. Preheat the oven to 180°C.
2. Cook the lentils according to the package instructions. Drain and set aside.
3. In a large frying pan, heat the olive oil over medium heat. Add the onion and garlic, and sauté until softened, about 5 minutes.
4. Add the carrots and courgette, and cook for another 5 minutes.
5. Stir in the chopped tomatoes, cooked lentils, dried thyme, and dried rosemary. Season with salt and black pepper. Simmer for 10 minutes.
6. Meanwhile, cook the potatoes in boiling water until tender. Drain and mash with a little olive oil or milk, if desired.
7. Transfer the lentil mixture to a baking dish and spread the mashed potatoes on top. Sprinkle with grated Cheddar cheese.
8. Bake for 20 minutes, until the top is golden and crispy.
9. Serve hot.

Nutrition Info per Serving:

Calories: 300, Protein: 15 g, Fat: 10 g, Carbohydrates: 40 g, Fibre: 8 g, Sugar: 7 g, Sodium: 280 mg

CHAPTER 8
Beans and Grains

Baked Falafel with Tahini Sauce

Serves: 4

PREP TIME: 15 minutes
COOK TIME: 20 minutes

400 g tinned chickpeas, drained and rinsed
1 onion, finely chopped
2 garlic cloves, minced
1 tbsp. ground cumin
1 tbsp. ground coriander
2 tbsps. fresh parsley, chopped
1 tbsp. olive oil
Salt and black pepper, to taste

For the Tahini Sauce:
3 tbsps. tahini
1 lemon, juiced
2 tbsps. water
1 garlic clove, minced
Salt to taste

1. Preheat the oven to 200°C. Line a baking tray with parchment paper.
2. In a food processor, combine the chickpeas, onion, garlic, cumin, coriander, parsley, olive oil, salt, and black pepper. Blend until smooth.
3. Form the mixture into small patties and place them on the prepared baking tray.
4. Bake for 20 minutes, turning halfway through, until golden and crispy.
5. For the tahini sauce, whisk together the tahini, lemon juice, water, garlic, and salt until smooth.
6. Serve the falafel hot with the tahini sauce.

Nutrition Info per Serving:

Calories: 220, Protein: 9 g, Fat: 11 g, Carbohydrates: 22 g, Fibre: 6 g, Sugar: 1 g, Sodium: 260 mg

Lemon and Herb Couscous

Serves: 4

PREP TIME: 20 minutes
COOK TIME: 0 minutes

200 g couscous
1 lemon, zested and juiced
2 tbsps. olive oil
1 cucumber, diced
1 red pepper, diced
50 g black olives, sliced
2 tbsps. fresh parsley, chopped
2 tbsps. fresh mint, chopped
Salt and black pepper, to taste

1. Place the couscous in a large bowl. Pour over 250 ml of boiling water. Cover and let sit for 10 minutes until the liquid is absorbed.
2. Fluff the couscous with a fork and stir in the lemon zest, lemon juice, and olive oil.
3. Add the diced cucumber, red pepper, and black olives. Toss to combine.
4. Garnish with fresh parsley and mint. Season with salt and black pepper.
5. Serve immediately.

Nutrition Info per Serving:

Calories: 180, Protein: 5 g, Fat: 8 g, Carbohydrates: 25 g, Fibre: 4 g, Sugar: 3 g, Sodium: 160 mg

CHAPTER 8
Beans and Grains

Greek Gigantes Beans

Serves: 4

300 g dried gigantes beans, soaked overnight
2 tbsps. olive oil
1 onion, finely chopped
2 garlic cloves, minced
1 tin of chopped tomatoes (400 g)
1 tbsp. tomato puree
1 tsp. dried oregano
1 tsp. dried thyme
Salt and black pepper, to taste
Fresh dill, chopped (for garnish)

PREP TIME: 15 minutes
COOK TIME: 50 minutes

1. Drain and rinse the soaked beans. Place them in a large pot, cover with water, and bring to a boil. Reduce the heat and simmer for 30 minutes, until tender. Drain and set aside.
2. In a large frying pan, heat the olive oil over medium heat. Add the onion and garlic, and sauté until softened, about 5 minutes.
3. Stir in the chopped tomatoes, tomato puree, dried oregano, and dried thyme. Season with salt and black pepper.
4. Add the cooked beans to the tomato mixture and simmer for another 15 minutes.
5. Garnish with fresh dill and serve hot.

Nutrition Info per Serving:

Calories: 240, Protein: 10 g, Fat: 8 g, Carbohydrates: 32 g, Fibre: 10 g, Sugar: 7 g, Sodium: 300 mg

Prawn and Asparagus Risotto

Serves: 4

200 g Arborio rice
2 tbsps. olive oil
1 onion, finely chopped
2 garlic cloves, minced
200 g prawns, peeled and deveined
200 g asparagus, chopped
1 litre vegetable stock
1 lemon, zested and juiced
50 g grated Parmesan cheese
Salt and black pepper, to taste
Fresh parsley, chopped (for garnish)

PREP TIME: 10 minutes
COOK TIME: 30 minutes

1. In a large pan, heat the olive oil over medium heat. Place the onion and garlic, and sauté until softened, about 5 minutes.
2. Stir in the Arborio rice and cook for 2 minutes until lightly toasted.
3. Gradually add the vegetable stock, one ladle at a time, stirring continuously until the liquid is absorbed before adding more.
4. After 15 minutes, add the prawns and asparagus. Cook for another 5-7 minutes, until the prawns are cooked and the asparagus is tender.
5. Stir in the lemon zest, lemon juice, and grated Parmesan cheese. Season with salt and black pepper.
6. Garnish with fresh parsley and serve hot.

Nutrition Info per Serving:

Calories: 320, Protein: 18 g, Fat: 10 g, Carbohydrates: 40 g, Fibre: 3 g, Sugar: 2 g, Sodium: 300 mg

Lentil and Mushroom Stuffed Cabbage Rolls

Serves: 4

|PREP TIME: 20 minutes
|COOK TIME: 40 minutes

8 large cabbage leaves
200 g cooked lentils
200 g mushrooms, finely chopped
1 onion, finely chopped
2 garlic cloves, minced
2 tbsps. olive oil
1 tin of chopped tomatoes (400 g)
1 tsp. dried thyme
1 tsp. dried rosemary
Salt and black pepper, to taste
Fresh parsley, chopped (for garnish)

1. Preheat the oven to 180°C.
2. Bring a large pot of water to a boil. Blanch the cabbage leaves for 2 minutes, until softened. Drain and set aside.
3. In a large frying pan, heat the olive oil over medium heat. Add the onion, garlic, and mushrooms, and sauté until softened, about 5 minutes.
4. Stir in the cooked lentils, dried thyme, and dried rosemary. Season with salt and black pepper.
5. Place a spoonful of the lentil mixture in the centre of each cabbage leaf. Roll up and place seam-side down in a baking dish.
6. Pour the chopped tomatoes over the cabbage rolls.
7. Bake for 30 minutes, until the cabbage is tender and the filling is heated through.
8. Garnish with fresh parsley and serve hot.

Nutrition Info per Serving:

Calories: 240, Protein: 10 g, Fat: 8 g, Carbohydrates: 34 g, Fibre: 10 g, Sugar: 8 g, Sodium: 260 mg

Tomato and Basil Barley

Serves: 4

|PREP TIME: 10 minutes
|COOK TIME: 30 minutes

2 tbsps. olive oil
200 g pearl barley
1 onion, finely chopped
2 garlic cloves, minced
400 g tinned chopped tomatoes
500 ml vegetable stock
1 tsp. dried basil
Salt and black pepper, to taste
Fresh basil, chopped (for garnish)

1. In a large pot over medium heat, heat the olive oil. Add the onion and garlic, and sauté until softened, about 3-5 minutes.
2. Stir in the pearl barley and cook for 2 minutes until lightly toasted.
3. Add the chopped tomatoes, vegetable stock, and dried basil. Bring to a boil, then reduce the heat and simmer for 25 minutes, until the barley is tender and the liquid is absorbed.
4. Garnish with fresh basil and season with salt and black pepper.
5. Serve hot.

Nutrition Info per Serving:

Calories: 210, Protein: 6 g, Fat: 8 g, Carbohydrates: 32 g, Fibre: 6 g, Sugar: 4 g, Sodium: 200 mg

CHAPTER 8
Beans and Grains

Spiced Rice with Chickpeas

Serves: 4

2 tbsps. olive oil
200 g basmati rice
1 onion, finely chopped
2 garlic cloves, minced
1 tin of chickpeas (400 g), drained and rinsed
1 tsp. ground cumin
1 tsp. ground coriander
1 tsp. ground turmeric
500 ml vegetable stock
Salt and black pepper, to taste
Fresh coriander, chopped (for garnish)

|**PREP TIME:** 10 minutes
|**COOK TIME:** 25 minutes

1. In a large pot, heat the olive oil over medium heat. Add the onion and garlic, and sauté until softened, about 5 minutes.
2. Stir in the chickpeas and spices, and cook for 2 minutes until fragrant.
3. Add the rice and cook for another 2 minutes until lightly toasted.
4. Pour in the vegetable stock and bring to a boil. Reduce the heat and simmer for 15 minutes, until the rice is tender and the liquid is absorbed.
5. Garnish with fresh coriander and season with salt and black pepper.
6. Serve hot.

Nutrition Info per Serving:

Calories: 240, Protein: 7 g, Fat: 8 g, Carbohydrates: 34 g, Fibre: 5 g, Sugar: 2 g, Sodium: 220 mg

Moroccan Spiced Lentils

Serves: 4

2 tbsps. olive oil
200 g red lentils
2 celery sticks, chopped
1 red pepper, chopped
1 onion, chopped
2 garlic cloves, minced
1 litre vegetable stock
1 tsp. ground cumin
1 tsp. ground coriander
1 tsp. ground cinnamon
1 tsp. smoked paprika
Salt and black pepper, to taste
Fresh coriander, chopped (for garnish)

|**PREP TIME:** 10 minutes
|**COOK TIME:** 30 minutes

1. In a large pot, heat the olive oil over medium-high heat. Add the onion and garlic, and sauté until softened, about 3-5 minutes.
2. Add the chopped celery and red pepper, and cook for another 5 minutes.
3. Stir in the red lentils, vegetable stock, ground cumin, ground coriander, ground cinnamon, and smoked paprika. Season with salt and black pepper.
4. Bring to a boil, then reduce the heat and simmer for 20 minutes, until the lentils are tender.
5. Garnish with fresh coriander and serve hot.

Nutrition Info per Serving:

Calories: 220, Protein: 10 g, Fat: 8 g, Carbohydrates: 30 g, Fibre: 9 g, Sugar: 6 g, Sodium: 260 mg

Roasted Vegetable Bulgur

Serves: 4

|PREP TIME: 15 minutes
|COOK TIME: 20 minutes

2 tbsps. olive oil
200 g bulgur wheat
1 courgette, diced
1 red pepper, diced
1 yellow pepper, diced
1 red onion, chopped
1 tsp. ground cumin
1 tsp. ground coriander
500 ml vegetable stock
Salt and black pepper, to taste
Fresh parsley, chopped (for garnish)

1. Preheat the oven to 200°C.
2. Place the diced courgette, red pepper, yellow pepper, and red onion on a baking tray. Drizzle with olive oil, season with ground cumin, ground coriander, salt, and black pepper. Toss to coat.
3. Roast the vegetables for 20 minutes, until tender and slightly charred.
4. Meanwhile, cook the bulgur wheat according to the package instructions. Drain and set aside.
5. In a large bowl, combine the roasted vegetables with the cooked bulgur wheat. Toss to combine.
6. Garnish with fresh parsley and serve hot.

Nutrition Info per Serving:

Calories: 220, Protein: 6 g, Fat: 9 g, Carbohydrates: 30 g, Fibre: 6 g, Sugar: 4 g, Sodium: 200 mg

Pea and Mint Orzo

Serves: 4

|PREP TIME: 10 minutes
|COOK TIME: 15-20 minutes

200 g orzo pasta
2 tbsps. olive oil
1 onion, finely chopped
2 garlic cloves, minced
200 g peas
1 lemon, zested and juiced
2 tbsps. fresh mint, chopped
Salt and black pepper, to taste
Fresh parsley, chopped (for garnish)

1. Cook the orzo pasta according to the package instructions. Drain and set aside.
2. In a large frying pan, heat the olive oil over medium heat. Add the onion and garlic, and sauté until softened, about 5 minutes.
3. Stir in the peas and cook for another 3-4 minutes, until heated through.
4. Add the cooked orzo, lemon zest, lemon juice, and fresh mint. Toss to combine.
5. Season with salt and black pepper.
6. Garnish with fresh parsley and serve hot.

Nutrition Info per Serving:

Calories: 220, Protein: 6 g, Fat: 10 g, Carbohydrates: 28 g, Fibre: 4 g, Sugar: 2 g, Sodium: 160 mg

CHAPTER 8
Beans and Grains

CHAPTER 9
Starters & Snacks

Roasted Red Pepper Hummus ·· 58

Courgette Fritters ·· 58

Cucumber Bites with Hummus ··· 59

Marinated Olives ··· 59

Tzatziki with Pitta Bread ··· 60

Baked Feta with Herbs ·· 60

Aubergine Caponata ··· 61

Tomato and Mozzarella Skewers ·· 61

Sun-dried Tomato and Pesto Pinwheels ·································· 62

Roasted Almonds with Rosemary ·· 62

Greek Spinach Pie ··· 63

Prawn and Avocado Cocktail ·· 63

Roasted Red Pepper Hummus

Serves: 4

PREP TIME: 10 minutes
COOK TIME: 10 minutes

1 tin of chickpeas (400 g), drained and rinsed
2 red peppers, roasted and chopped
2 tbsps. tahini
2 garlic cloves, minced
2 tbsps. olive oil
1 tbsp. lemon juice
Salt and black pepper, to taste

1. In a food processor, combine the chickpeas, roasted red peppers, tahini, garlic, olive oil, and lemon juice.
2. Blend until smooth. Season with salt and black pepper.
3. Serve with pitta bread or vegetable sticks.

Nutrition Info per Serving:

Calories: 180, Protein: 6 g, Fat: 10 g, Carbohydrates: 18 g, Fibre: 5 g, Sugar: 3 g, Sodium: 200 mg

Courgette Fritters

Serves: 4

PREP TIME: 20 minutes
COOK TIME: 15 minutes

2 large courgettes, grated
1 onion, finely chopped
2 garlic cloves, minced
2 tbsps. olive oil
1 egg, beaten
50 g wholemeal flour
1 tsp. dried oregano
Salt and black pepper, to taste
Greek yoghurt, for serving

1. Place the grated courgettes in a colander, sprinkle with salt, and let drain for 10 minutes. Squeeze out excess moisture.
2. In a large bowl, combine the courgettes, onion, garlic, beaten egg, wholemeal flour, and dried oregano. Season with salt and black pepper.
3. Heat the olive oil in a frying pan over medium heat. Drop spoonfuls of the courgette mixture into the pan, flattening them slightly.
4. Cook for 3-4 minutes on each side, until golden brown.
5. Serve with Greek yoghurt.

Nutrition Info per Serving:

Calories: 160, Protein: 4 g, Fat: 10 g, Carbohydrates: 14 g, Fibre: 3 g, Sugar: 2 g, Sodium: 180 mg

CHAPTER 8
Beans and Grains

Cucumber Bites with Hummus

Serves: 4

1 large cucumber, sliced into rounds
200 g hummus
1 red pepper, finely chopped
1 tbsp. fresh parsley, chopped
Salt and black pepper, to taste

PREP TIME: 10 minutes
COOK TIME: 0 minutes

1. Arrange the cucumber slices on a serving platter.
2. Top each cucumber slice with a spoonful of hummus.
3. Sprinkle the finely chopped red pepper and fresh parsley over the hummus.
4. Season with salt and black pepper.
5. Serve immediately.

Nutrition Info per Serving:

Calories: 90, Protein: 3 g, Fat: 5 g, Carbohydrates: 9 g, Fibre: 3 g, Sugar: 2 g, Sodium: 180 mg

Marinated Olives

Serves: 4

200 g mixed olives
2 tbsps. olive oil
1 garlic clove, minced
1 tsp. dried oregano
1 tsp. dried thyme
1 lemon, zested
Fresh rosemary, chopped (for garnish)
Salt and black pepper, to taste

PREP TIME: 5 minutes
COOK TIME: 0 minutes

1. In a bowl, combine the mixed olives, olive oil, garlic, dried oregano, dried thyme, and lemon zest. Season with salt and black pepper.
2. Garnish with fresh rosemary.
3. Serve immediately or marinate in the fridge for 1-2 hours for more flavour.

Nutrition Info per Serving:

Calories: 180, Protein: 1 g, Fat: 16 g, Carbohydrates: 6 g, Fibre: 3 g, Sugar: 0 g, Sodium: 400 mg

Tzatziki with Pitta Bread

Serves: 4

PREP TIME: 15 minutes
COOK TIME: 0 minutes

200 g Greek yoghurt
1 cucumber, grated and drained
2 garlic cloves, minced
1 tbsp. olive oil
1 tbsp. lemon juice
1 tbsp. fresh dill, chopped
Salt and black pepper, to taste
4 wholemeal pitta breads, warmed and sliced

1. In a bowl, combine the Greek yoghurt, grated cucumber, minced garlic, olive oil, lemon juice, and fresh dill. Season with salt and black pepper.
2. Serve the tzatziki with warm wholemeal pitta bread slices.

Nutrition Info per Serving:

Calories: 180, Protein: 8 g, Fat: 6 g, Carbohydrates: 22 g, Fibre: 4 g, Sugar: 5 g, Sodium: 220 mg

Baked Feta with Herbs

Serves: 4

PREP TIME: 5 minutes
COOK TIME: 20 minutes

200 g feta cheese
2 tbsps. olive oil
1 tsp. dried oregano
1 tsp. dried thyme
1 lemon, sliced
Fresh parsley, chopped (for garnish)
Wholemeal bread, for serving

1. Preheat the oven to 180°C.
2. Place the feta cheese in a small baking dish. Drizzle with olive oil and sprinkle with dried oregano and dried thyme. Arrange the lemon slices around the feta.
3. Bake for 20 minutes, until the feta is soft and slightly golden.
4. Garnish with fresh parsley and serve with wholemeal bread.

Nutrition Info per Serving:

Calories: 210, Protein: 7 g, Fat: 18 g, Carbohydrates: 4 g, Fibre: 1 g, Sugar: 0 g, Sodium: 320 mg

CHAPTER 8
Beans and Grains

Aubergine Caponata

Serves: 4

2 tbsps. olive oil
1 large aubergine, diced
1 onion, chopped
2 garlic cloves, minced
2 celery sticks, chopped
200 g cherry tomatoes, halved

2 tbsps. capers
50 g black olives, sliced
1 tbsp. red wine vinegar
1 tsp. dried oregano
Salt and black pepper, to taste
Fresh basil, chopped (for garnish)

|**PREP TIME:** 10 minutes
|**COOK TIME:** 25 minutes

1. In a large frying pan, heat the olive oil over medium heat. Add the aubergine and cook until golden and tender, about 10 minutes.
2. Add the onion, garlic, and celery, and cook for another 5 minutes.
3. Stir in the cherry tomatoes, capers, black olives, red wine vinegar, and dried oregano. Season with salt and black pepper.
4. Simmer for 10 minutes, until the vegetables are tender and the flavours are combined.
5. Garnish with fresh basil and serve hot or cold.

Nutrition Info per Serving:

Calories: 180, Protein: 3 g, Fat: 12 g, Carbohydrates: 18 g, Fibre: 6 g, Sugar: 7 g, Sodium: 300 mg

Tomato and Mozzarella Skewers

Serves: 4

200 g cherry tomatoes
200 g fresh mozzarella balls
1 bunch fresh basil leaves
2 tbsps. olive oil
1 tbsp. balsamic vinegar
Salt and black pepper, to taste

|**PREP TIME:** 10 minutes
|**COOK TIME:** 0 minutes

1. Thread the cherry tomatoes, mozzarella balls, and fresh basil leaves onto skewers, alternating between them.
2. In a small bowl, whisk together the olive oil and balsamic vinegar.
3. Drizzle the skewers with the dressing and season with salt and black pepper.
4. Serve immediately.

Nutrition Info per Serving:

Calories: 140, Protein: 7 g, Fat: 10 g, Carbohydrates: 4 g, Fibre: 1 g, Sugar: 2 g, Sodium: 180 mg

Sun-dried Tomato and Pesto Pinwheels

Serves: 4

PREP TIME: 15 minutes
COOK TIME: 10 minutes

1 sheet ready-rolled puff pastry
4 tbsps. pesto
50 g sun-dried tomatoes, chopped
50 g grated Parmesan cheese
1 egg, beaten

1. Preheat the oven to 200°C.
2. Roll out the puff pastry sheet and spread an even layer of pesto over it.
3. Sprinkle the chopped sun-dried tomatoes and grated Parmesan cheese over the pesto.
4. Roll the pastry sheet tightly into a log and cut into 1 cm thick slices.
5. Place the pinwheels on a baking tray lined with parchment paper. Brush with beaten egg.
6. Bake for 10 minutes, until golden brown.
7. Serve warm or at room temperature.

Nutrition Info per Serving:

Calories: 220, Protein: 6 g, Fat: 16 g, Carbohydrates: 14 g, Fibre: 1 g, Sugar: 1 g, Sodium: 280 mg

Roasted Almonds with Rosemary

Serves: 4

PREP TIME: 5 minutes
COOK TIME: 15 minutes

200 g raw almonds
1 tbsp. olive oil
1 tbsp. fresh rosemary, chopped
½ tsp. sea salt

1. Preheat the oven to 180°C.
2. In a bowl, toss the almonds with olive oil, chopped rosemary, and sea salt.
3. Spread the almonds in a single layer on a baking tray.
4. Roast for 15 minutes, stirring occasionally, until the almonds are golden and fragrant.
5. Allow to cool before serving.

Nutrition Info per Serving:

Calories: 200, Protein: 7 g, Fat: 18 g, Carbohydrates: 6 g, Fibre: 4 g, Sugar: 1 g, Sodium: 120 mg

Greek Spinach Pie

Serves: 4

200 g fresh spinach, chopped
1 onion, finely chopped
2 garlic cloves, minced
200 g feta cheese, crumbled
2 eggs, beaten
2 tbsps. olive oil
1 tsp. dried dill
Salt and black pepper, to taste
4 sheets of filo pastry

PREP TIME: 15 minutes
COOK TIME: 35 minutes

1. Preheat the oven to 180°C.
2. In a frying pan, heat 1 tbsp. of olive oil over medium heat. Add the onion and garlic, and sauté until softened, about 5 minutes.
3. Stir in the chopped spinach and cook until wilted, about 3 minutes.
4. In a bowl, combine the spinach mixture, crumbled feta cheese, beaten eggs, and dried dill. Season with salt and black pepper.
5. Brush each sheet of filo pastry with the remaining olive oil. Layer the sheets in a baking dish.
6. Spread the spinach mixture over the filo pastry. Fold the edges of the pastry over the filling.
7. Bake for 25-30 minutes, until the pastry is golden and crispy.
8. Serve hot.

Nutrition Info per Serving:

Calories: 250, Protein: 10 g, Fat: 16 g, Carbohydrates: 18 g, Fibre: 2 g, Sugar: 2 g, Sodium: 300 mg

Prawn and Avocado Cocktail

Serves: 4

200 g cooked prawns
2 ripe avocados, diced
1 cucumber, diced
1 red onion, finely chopped
2 tbsps. olive oil
1 tbsp. lemon juice
1 tbsp. fresh coriander, chopped
Salt and black pepper, to taste

PREP TIME: 15 minutes
COOK TIME: 5 minutes

1. In a large bowl, combine the cooked prawns, diced avocados, cucumber, and red onion.
2. Drizzle with olive oil and lemon juice. Toss to combine.
3. Season with salt and black pepper.
4. Garnish with fresh coriander and serve immediately.

Nutrition Info per Serving:

Calories: 200, Protein: 14 g, Fat: 14 g, Carbohydrates: 6 g, Fibre: 4 g, Sugar: 1 g, Sodium: 240 mg

CHAPTER 8
Beans and Grains

CHAPTER 10
Desserts & Drinks

Watermelon and Mint Cooler ········· 65

Sparkling Lemonade with Rosemary ········· 65

Orange Cake ········· 66

Almond and Lemon Biscotti ········· 66

Pears Poached in Red Wine ········· 67

Ricotta and Berry Parfaits ········· 67

Greek Yoghurt with Honey and Nuts ········· 68

Fig and Almond Tart ········· 68

Hibiscus Iced Tea ········· 69

Strawberry and Basil Lemonade ········· 69

Cucumber and Lemon Detox Drink ········· 70

Pomegranate and Mint Spritzer ········· 70

Watermelon and Mint Cooler

Serves: 4

500 g watermelon, cubed
1 tbsp. lime juice
1 tbsp. honey
200 ml cold water
Fresh mint leaves

PREP TIME: 10 minutes
COOK TIME: 0 minutes

1. In a blender, combine the watermelon, lime juice, honey, and cold water. Blend until smooth.
2. Strain the mixture through a fine mesh sieve to remove any pulp.
3. Serve over ice, garnished with fresh mint leaves.

Nutrition Info per Serving:

Calories: 50, Protein: 1 g, Fat: 0 g, Carbohydrates: 12 g, Fibre: 1 g, Sugar: 10 g, Sodium: 5 mg

Sparkling Lemonade with Rosemary

Serves: 4

200 ml fresh lemon juice
1 litre sparkling water
2 tbsps. honey
2 sprigs fresh rosemary

PREP TIME: 5 minutes
COOK TIME: 5 minutes

1. In a small saucepan, combine the lemon juice, honey, and fresh rosemary. Bring to a simmer and cook for 5 minutes.
2. Remove from heat and let cool to room temperature. Remove the rosemary sprigs.
3. In a large jug, combine the lemon mixture with sparkling water.
4. Serve over ice.

Nutrition Info per Serving:

Calories: 50, Protein: 0 g, Fat: 0 g, Carbohydrates: 13 g, Fibre: 0 g, Sugar: 12 g, Sodium: 10 mg

CHAPTER 10
Desserts & Drinks

Orange Cake

Serves: 8

PREP TIME: 15 minutes
COOK TIME: 35 minutes

200 g almond flour
1 tsp. baking powder
½ tsp. bicarbonate of soda
150 g caster sugar
2 large eggs
120 ml olive oil
120 ml fresh orange juice
Zest of 1 orange
1 tsp. vanilla extract

1. Preheat the oven to 180°C. Grease and flour a 20 cm cake tin.
2. In a bowl, combine the flour, baking powder, and bicarbonate of soda.
3. In a separate bowl, whisk the sugar and eggs until pale and fluffy. Gradually add the olive oil, orange juice, orange zest, and vanilla extract.
4. Fold the dry ingredients into the wet mixture until well combined.
5. Pour the batter into the prepared cake tin and bake for 35 minutes, or until a toothpick inserted into the centre comes out clean.
6. Allow the cake to cool before serving.

Nutrition Info per Serving:

Calories: 250, Protein: 4 g, Fat: 14 g, Carbohydrates: 30 g, Fibre: 1 g, Sugar: 16 g, Sodium: 100 mg

Almond and Lemon Biscotti

Serves: 12

PREP TIME: 30 minutes
COOK TIME: 40 minutes

200 g almond flour
100 g caster sugar
1 tsp. baking powder
2 large eggs
100 g almonds, chopped
Zest of 1 lemon
1 tsp. vanilla extract

1. Preheat the oven to 180°C. Line a baking tray with parchment paper.
2. In a bowl, combine the flour, sugar, and baking powder.
3. In a separate bowl, whisk the eggs, then add to the dry ingredients along with the almonds, lemon zest, and vanilla extract. Mix until a dough forms.
4. Divide the dough in half and shape each half into a log about 30 cm long. Place the logs on the baking tray and flatten slightly.
5. Bake for 25 minutes, until lightly golden. Remove from the oven and allow to cool for 10 minutes.
6. Cut the logs into 1 cm thick slices and place them back on the baking tray, cut side up.
7. Bake for another 15 minutes, until the biscotti are crisp and golden.
8. Allow to cool before serving.

Nutrition Info per Serving:

Calories: 140, Protein: 4 g, Fat: 6 g, Carbohydrates: 18 g, Fibre: 2 g, Sugar: 10 g, Sodium: 50 mg

Pears Poached in Red Wine

Serves: 4

2 wholemeal bagels
100 g smoked salmon
100 g light soft cheese
1 tbsp. capers
1 small red onion, thinly sliced
1 tbsp. fresh dill, chopped
Lemon wedges, to serve

PREP TIME: 10 minutes
COOK TIME: 25 minutes

1. In a large saucepan, combine the red wine, sugar, cinnamon stick, vanilla pod, and orange zest. Bring to a boil, stirring until the sugar is dissolved.
2. Add the pears and reduce the heat to a simmer.
3. Cook the pears for 20-25 minutes, turning occasionally, until they are tender.
4. Remove the pears from the saucepan and set aside.
5. Continue to simmer the liquid until it reduces to a syrupy consistency.
6. Serve the pears drizzled with the red wine syrup.

Nutrition Info per Serving:

Calories: 180, Protein: 1 g, Fat: 0 g, Carbohydrates: 35 g, Fibre: 5 g, Sugar: 32 g, Sodium: 10 mg

Ricotta and Berry Parfaits

Serves: 4

250 g ricotta cheese
2 tbsps. honey
200 g mixed berries (strawberries, blueberries, raspberries)
50 g granola
Fresh mint leaves (for garnish)

PREP TIME: 10 minutes
COOK TIME: 0 minutes

1. In a bowl, mix the ricotta cheese and honey until smooth.
2. In serving glasses, layer the ricotta mixture, mixed berries, and granola.
3. Repeat the layers, finishing with a layer of berries and granola on top.
4. Garnish with fresh mint leaves.
5. Serve immediately.

Nutrition Info per Serving:

Calories: 200, Protein: 8 g, Fat: 10 g, Carbohydrates: 20 g, Fibre: 4 g, Sugar: 14 g, Sodium: 70 mg

CHAPTER 10
Desserts & Drinks

Greek Yoghurt with Honey and Nuts

Serves: 2

|PREP TIME: 5 minutes
|COOK TIME: 0 minutes

400 g Greek yoghurt
2 tbsps. honey
30 g mixed nuts, chopped
1 tbsp. chia seeds (optional)
Fresh berries (optional)

1. Divide the Greek yoghurt evenly between two bowls.
2. Drizzle 1 tbsp. of honey over each bowl of yoghurt.
3. Sprinkle the chopped nuts and chia seeds (if using) on top.
4. Add fresh berries for extra flavour and nutrients, if desired.
5. Serve immediately.

Nutrition Info per Serving:

Calories: 180, Protein: 12 g, Fat: 8 g, Carbohydrates: 15 g, Fibre: 2 g, Sugar: 13 g, Sodium: 55 mg

Fig and Almond Tart

Serves: 8

|PREP TIME: 20 minutes
|COOK TIME: 30 minutes

Cooking spray
200 g almond flour
100 g cold butter, cubed
50 g caster sugar
1 egg yolk
2-3 tbsps. cold water
200 g fresh figs, sliced
50 g ground almonds
2 tbsps. honey

1. Preheat the oven to 180°C. Grease a 23 cm tart tin with cooking spray.
2. In a bowl, rub the butter into the flour until the mixture resembles breadcrumbs. Stir in the sugar.
3. Add the egg yolk and enough cold water to bring the mixture together into a dough.
4. Roll out the dough on a floured surface and line the tart tin. Trim the edges.
5. Spread the ground almonds evenly over the base of the tart.
6. Arrange the fig slices on top of the almonds.
7. Drizzle with honey.
8. Bake for 30 minutes, until the pastry is golden and the figs are tender.
9. Allow to cool before serving.

Nutrition Info per Serving:

Calories: 250, Protein: 5 g, Fat: 12 g, Carbohydrates: 32 g, Fibre: 3 g, Sugar: 16 g, Sodium: 50 mg

CHAPTER 10
Desserts & Drinks

Hibiscus Iced Tea

Serves: 4

4 hibiscus tea bags
1 litre boiling water
1 tbsp. honey
1 lime, sliced

|PREP TIME: 15 minutes, plus 2 hours chilling time
|COOK TIME: 0 minutes

1. Place the hibiscus tea bags in a large heatproof jug and pour over the boiling water.
2. Stir in the honey and add the lime slices.
3. Let the tea steep for 10 minutes, then remove the tea bags and let the tea cool to room temperature.
4. Chill in the fridge for at least 2 hours.
5. Serve over ice.

Nutrition Info per Serving:

Calories: 25, Protein: 0 g, Fat: 0 g, Carbohydrates: 6 g, Fibre: 0 g, Sugar: 6 g, Sodium: 0 mg

Strawberry and Basil Lemonade

Serves: 4

200 g strawberries, hulled and sliced
200 ml fresh lemon juice
1 litre cold water
2 tbsps. honey
Fresh basil leaves

|PREP TIME: 10 minutes
|COOK TIME: 0 minutes

1. In a blender, combine the strawberries, lemon juice, and honey. Blend until smooth.
2. In a large jug, combine the strawberry mixture with cold water.
3. Serve over ice with fresh basil leaves.

Nutrition Info per Serving:

Calories: 50, Protein: 1 g, Fat: 0 g, Carbohydrates: 13 g, Fibre: 1 g, Sugar: 10 g, Sodium: 5 mg

Cucumber and Lemon Detox Drink

Serves: 4

PREP TIME: 5 minutes, plus 30 minutes for infusing
COOK TIME: 0 minutes

1 litre cold water
1 cucumber, sliced
1 lemon, sliced
Fresh mint leaves

1. In a large jug, combine the cold water, cucumber slices, and lemon slices.
2. Let the mixture infuse for at least 30 minutes in the fridge.
3. Serve chilled with fresh mint leaves.

Nutrition Info per Serving:

Calories: 5, Protein: 0 g, Fat: 0 g, Carbohydrates: 1 g, Fibre: 0 g, Sugar: 0 g, Sodium: 0 mg

Pomegranate and Mint Spritzer

Serves: 4

PREP TIME: 5 minutes
COOK TIME: 0 minutes

500 ml pomegranate juice
500 ml sparkling water
1 tbsp. lemon juice
Fresh mint leaves
Pomegranate seeds (for garnish)

1. In a large jug, combine the pomegranate juice, sparkling water, and lemon juice.
2. Add fresh mint leaves and stir gently.
3. Serve over ice, garnished with pomegranate seeds.

Nutrition Info per Serving:

Calories: 60, Protein: 0 g, Fat: 0 g, Carbohydrates: 15 g, Fibre: 1 g, Sugar: 14 g, Sodium: 5 mg

Appendix 1: Measurement Conversion Chart

WEIGHT EQUIVALENTS

METRIC	US STANDARD	US STANDARD (OUNCES)
15 g	1 tablespoon	1/2 ounce
30 g	1/8 cup	1 ounce
60 g	1/4 cup	2 ounces
115 g	1/2 cup	4 ounces
170 g	3/4 cup	6 ounces
225 g	1 cup	8 ounces
450 g	2 cups	16 ounces
900 g	4 cups	2 pounds

VOLUME EQUIVALENTS

METRIC	US STANDARD	US STANDARD (OUNCES)
15 ml	1 tablespoon	1/2 fl.oz.
30 ml	2 tablespoons	1 fl.oz.
60 ml	1/4 cup	2 fl.oz.
125 ml	1/2 cup	4 fl.oz.
180 ml	3/4 cup	6 fl.oz.
250 ml	1 cup	8 fl.oz.
500 ml	2 cups	16 fl.oz.
1000 ml	4 cups	1 quart

TEMPERATURES EQUIVALENTS

CELSIUS (C)	FAHRENHEIT (F) (APPROXIMATE)
120 °C	250 °F
135 °C	275 °F
150 °C	300 °F
160 °C	325 °F
175 °C	350 °F
190 °C	375 °F
205 °C	400 °F
220 °C	425 °F
230 °C	450 °F
245°C	475 °F
260 °C	500 °F

LENGTH EQUIVALENTS

METRIC	IMPERIAL
3 mm	1/8 inch
6 mm	1/4 inch
1 cm	1/2 inch
2.5 cm	1 inch
3 cm	1 1/4 inches
5 cm	2 inches
10 cm	4 inches
15 cm	6 inches
20 cm	8 inches

Appendix 2: 30-Day Meal Plan

Meal Plan	Breakfast	Lunch	Dinner	Snack/Dessert
Day-1	Mediterranean Chickpea Pancakes	Lemon and Herb Couscous	Grilled Lamb and Vegetable Kebabs	Sun-dried Tomato and Pesto Pinwheels
Day-2	Avocado and Tomato on Wholemeal Toast	Garlic Prawns with Spinach	Fennel and Leek Soup	Roasted Almonds with Rosemary
Day-3	Mediterranean Breakfast Quinoa	Spinach and Ricotta Cannelloni	Beef and Pepper Skewers	Strawberry and Basil Lemonade
Day-4	Roasted Tomato and Basil Porridge	Chicken Souvlaki	Rocket and Parmesan Salad	Pears Poached in Red Wine
Day-5	Mediterranean-style Scrambled Eggs	Vegan Moussaka	Prawn and Asparagus Risotto	Marinated Olives
Day-6	Aubergine and Red Pepper Shakshuka	Mediterranean Pork Chops	Tabbouleh Salad	Orange Cake
Day-7	Mediterranean Vegetable Frittata	Spanish Gazpacho	Greek Lemon Chicken	Cucumber Bites with Hummus
Day-8	Tomato and Olive Breakfast Muffins	Herb-Roasted Turkey Breast	Courgette and Tomato Gratin	Almond and Lemon Biscotti
Day-9	Courgette and Ricotta Tart	Mussels in White Wine Sauce	Moroccan Spiced Lentils	Tzatziki with Pitta Bread
Day-10	Spinach and Feta Omelette	Grilled Calamari with Garlic and Lemon	Pork Medallions with Balsamic Glaze	Ricotta and Berry Parfaits

Meal Plan	Breakfast	Lunch	Dinner	Snack/Dessert
Day-11	Smoked Salmon and Soft Cheese Bagel	Seafood Linguine with Cherry Tomatoes	Stuffed Chicken Breasts with Spinach and Feta	Courgette Fritters
Day-12	Courgette and Ricotta Tart	Lamb and Spinach Curry	Sardines with Roasted Vegetables	Greek Yoghurt with Honey and Nuts
Day-13	Mediterranean Chickpea Pancakes	Greek Gigantes Beans	Grilled Sea Bass with Lemon and Herbs	Tomato and Mozzarella Skewers
Day-14	Roasted Pepper and Goat's Cheese Toast	Beef and Tomato Stuffed Peppers	Fennel and Leek Soup	Tzatziki with Pitta Bread
Day-15	Mediterranean Vegetable Frittata	Spinach and Ricotta Cannelloni	Chicken Souvlaki	Pomegranate and Mint Spritzer
Day-16	Spinach and Feta Omelette	Greek Lemon Chicken	Courgette and Tomato Gratin	Sun-dried Tomato and Pesto Pinwheels
Day-17	Aubergine and Red Pepper Shakshuka	Garlic Prawns with Spinach	Caprese Salad	Almond and Lemon Biscotti
Day-18	Avocado and Tomato on Wholemeal Toast	Rocket and Parmesan Salad	Pork Medallions with Balsamic Glaze	Roasted Almonds with Rosemary
Day-19	Mediterranean Breakfast Quinoa	Butternut Squash and Chickpea Tagine	Mediterranean Black Bean Tacos	Fig and Almond Tart
Day-20	Roasted Tomato and Basil Porridge	Tabbouleh Salad	Grilled Lamb and Vegetable Kebabs	Orange Cake

APPENDIX

Meal Plan	Breakfast	Lunch	Dinner	Snack/Dessert
Day-21	Tomato and Olive Breakfast Muffins	Sardines with Roasted Vegetables	Herb-Roasted Turkey Breast	Cucumber Bites with Hummus
Day-22	Mediterranean Vegetable Frittata	Lamb and Spinach Curry	Caprese Salad	Ricotta and Berry Parfaits
Day-23	Roasted Pepper and Goat's Cheese Toast	Prawn and Asparagus Risotto	Butternut Squash and Chickpea Tagine	Pears Poached in Red Wine
Day-24	Courgette and Ricotta Tart	Grilled Sea Bass with Lemon and Herbs	Lemon and Herb Couscous	Pomegranate and Mint Spritzer
Day-25	Roasted Tomato and Basil Porridge	Moroccan Spiced Lentils	Seafood Linguine with Cherry Tomatoes	Courgette Fritters
Day-26	Mediterranean-style Scrambled Eggs	Grilled Calamari with Garlic and Lemon	Vegan Moussaka	Strawberry and Basil Lemonade
Day-27	Smoked Salmon and Soft Cheese Bagel	Stuffed Chicken Breasts with Spinach and Feta	Greek Gigantes Beans	Greek Yoghurt with Honey and Nuts
Day-28	Spinach and Feta Omelette	Mediterranean Pork Chops	Spanish Gazpacho	Tomato and Mozzarella Skewers
Day-29	Mediterranean Chickpea Pancakes	Mussels in White Wine Sauce	Mediterranean Black Bean Tacos	Fig and Almond Tart
Day-30	Avocado and Tomato on Wholemeal Toast	Artichoke and Potato Stew	Beef and Pepper Skewers	Marinated Olives

Appendix 3: Recipes Index

A

ALMOND
Roasted Almonds with Rosemary — 62
Almond and Lemon Biscotti — 66

ARTICHOKE
Artichoke and Sun-dried Tomato Salad — 42

AUBERGINE
Aubergine and Red Pepper Shakshuka — 12
Vegan Moussaka — 15
Stuffed Aubergines with Quinoa — 18
Grilled Aubergine Rolls — 19
Aubergine and Tomato Stew — 48
Aubergine Caponata — 61

AVOCADO
Avocado and Tomato on Wholemeal Toast — 8
Quinoa and Avocado Salad — 37

B

BABY CUCUMBER
Mediterranean Breakfast Quinoa — 13

BEAN
Greek Gigantes Beans — 53

BEEF MINCE
Beef and Aubergine Moussaka — 29
Beef and Tomato Stuffed Peppers — 30

BERRIES
Ricotta and Berry Parfaits — 67

BLACK BEAN
Mediterranean Black Bean Tacos — 51

BUTTERNUT SQUASH
Butternut Squash and Chickpea Tagine — 16

C

CABBAGE
Lentil and Mushroom Stuffed Cabbage Rolls — 54

CALAMARI
Grilled Calamari with Garlic and Lemon — 26

CANNELLINI BEAN
White Bean and Spinach Soup — 49

CARROT
Spiced Carrot and Lentil Soup — 44

CELERY
Italian Minestrone — 47

CHERRY TOMATO
Mediterranean Vegetable Frittata — 8
Roasted Tomato and Basil Porridge — 10
Tomato and Olive Breakfast Muffins — 11
Vegan Pesto Pasta — 39
Tomato and Mozzarella Skewers — 61

CHICKEN
Greek Lemon Chicken Soup — 46

CHICKEN BREAST
Chicken Souvlaki — 33
Stuffed Chicken Breasts with Spinach and Feta — 34
Chicken and Artichoke Stew — 35

CHICKEN THIGH
Greek Lemon Chicken — 46

CHICKPEA
Chickpea and Spinach Stew — 46
Baked Falafel with Tahini Sauce — 52
Spiced Rice with Chickpeas — 55
Roasted Red Pepper Hummus — 58

COD
Baked Cod with Tomatoes and Olives — 22
Seafood Cioppino — 48

COURGETTE
Courgette and Ricotta Tart — 13
Grilled Vegetable Skewers with Tzatziki — 16
Vegan Mediterranean Pizza — 19

Roasted Vegetable Couscous 20
Pesto Pasta with Roasted Vegetables 40
Roasted Vegetable Bulgur 56
Courgette Fritters 58
CUCUMBER
Lemon and Herb Couscous 52
Cucumber Bites with Hummus 59
Tzatziki with Pitta Bread 60
Cucumber and Lemon Detox Drink 70

F-L

FIG
Fig and Almond Tart 68
LAMB LEG
Grilled Lamb and Vegetable Kebabs 32
LAMB MINCE
Lamb Koftas 33
LAMB SHOULDER
Lamb and Spinach Curry 32
LEEK
Fennel and Leek Soup 45
LEMON
Spaghetti with Lemon and Capers 40
Baked Feta with Herbs 60

M

MUSHROOM
Mushroom and Thyme Spelt 18
MUSSEL
Mediterranean Seafood Paella 24
Mussels in White Wine Sauce 25

N

NUT
Greek Yoghurt with Honey and Nuts 68

O

OCTOPUS
Grilled Octopus with Lemon Potatoes 23
OLIVE
Marinated Olives 59

P

PEA
Pea and Mint Orzo 56
PEAR
Pears Poached in Red Wine 67
PEPPER
Roasted Pepper and Goat's Cheese Toast 12
POMEGRANATE
Pomegranate and Mint Spritzer 70
PORK CHOP
Mediterranean Pork Chops 31
PORK MINCE
Pork and Fennel Meatballs 30
PORK TENDERLOIN
Pork Medallions with Balsamic Glaze 31
POTATO
Artichoke and Potato Stew 44
PRAWN
Garlic Prawns with Spinach 24
Seafood Linguine with Cherry Tomatoes 39
Prawn and Asparagus Risotto 53
Prawn and Avocado Cocktail 63
PUMPKIN
Pumpkin and Red Pepper Soup 49

R

RED LENTIL
Lentil and Vegetable Soup 17
Moroccan Spiced Lentils 55
Lentil and Vegetable Shepherd's Pie 51

RED PEPPER

Mediterranean Chickpea Pancakes	9
Mediterranean Stuffed Peppers	15
Roasted Red Pepper and Olive Salad	41

ROCKET

Rocket and Parmesan Salad	37

S

SARDINE

Sardines with Roasted Vegetables	25

SEA BASS

Grilled Sea Bass with Lemon and Herbs	22

SIRLOIN STEAK

Beef and Pepper Skewers	29

SMOKED SALMON

Smoked Salmon and Soft Cheese Bagel	9

SPINACH

Spinach and Feta Omelette	10
Mediterranean-style Scrambled Eggs	11
Spinach and Ricotta Cannelloni	38
Greek Spinach Pie	63

STRAWBERRY

Strawberry and Basil Lemonade	69

SUN-DRIED TOMATO

Mediterranean Penne with Sun-dried Tomatoes	38
Sun-dried Tomato and Pesto Pinwheels	62

T

TOMATO

Mediterranean Stuffed Tomatoes	17
Courgette and Tomato Gratin	20
Caprese Salad	41
Tabbouleh Salad	42
Spanish Gazpacho	45
Tomato and Basil Soup	47
Tomato and Basil Barley	54

TROUT

Baked Trout with Almonds and Herbs	27

TUNA

Mediterranean Tuna Steak	23

TURKEY BREAST

Herb-Roasted Turkey Breast	34

W

WATERMELON

Watermelon and Mint Cooler	65

WHITE FISH

Fish Kebabs with Vegetables	26
Mediterranean-style Fish Tacos	27